Leckie✗Leckie
Scotland's leading educational publishers

Success guides

Intermediate 2
Geography

✗ Rob Hands ✗

Contents

Making a Start

Graphs

Physical Environments

Map Skills

Human Environments

Contents

Environmental Interactions

How to use this Success Guide

This *Success Guide* is designed to help you revise for the examination, prelim and NAB (National Assessment Bank) tests you will meet on the way through your Intermediate 2 Geography course, and to give you guidance on answering questions. It will attempt to help you not only gain a basic pass, but build on that and secure a good grade – perhaps even a grade A. Remember though, most of your geography work has been done in class and is based on class notes and perhaps a textbook, as well as the support of your teacher. This guide does not purport to cover every topic in depth and, besides that, the examples used may not be the case-studies with which you are familiar. Instead, it should provide guidance and hints, such as those found in the **Top Tips**, to help your preparation. It also provides you with an outline of the course that details what you are expected to know. Beyond that, it will give you the opportunity to complete **Quick Tests** as a spot check on your progress while **exam-style questions**, with suggestions about how they might be tackled, will give you practice for the real examination.

Your Intermediate 2 Geography course

In your Intermediate 2 Geography course you will cover a wide range of topics. These are contained in three **units** which will be tested in NAB tests as the course progresses and in the examination at the end of the course. It is very likely that you will have a prelim exam that follows the format of the final exam.

Geography: Physical Environments unit

This unit is based on the British Isles and involves the study of how landscapes are formed by agents of erosion such as glaciers, rivers and the sea. It explains how limestone landscapes (karst) are formed by chemical weathering and how physical weathering affects the landscape. The ways in which people interact with these environments are also part of this unit.

Geography: Human Environments unit

This unit has a wider context and uses case-studies from the **Economically More Developed Countries (EMDCs)** and the **Economically Less Developed Countries (ELDCs).** The topics covered include world population characteristics, urban areas in rich and poor countries, industrial development and contrasts in farming.

Geography: Environmental Interactions unit

This unit has an emphasis on global issues. You will cover **two** out of five interaction topics for the exam.

Interaction 1: rural land degradation

This study excludes the British Isles and involves two examples of land degradation, one involving deforestation and one involving desertification of arid and semi-arid areas.

Interaction 2: river basin management

This study has a global context outside Europe and involves a detailed study of one river basin.

Interaction 3: european environmental inequalities

This study naturally has a European context in which case-studies involving environmental issues are drawn from more than one country. One of these must be from the European mainland.

Interaction 4: development and health

This study is done in a global context and is based on similarities and differences between EMDCs and ELDCs in terms of both development and health. It also involves a case-study of two different diseases, one from an EMDC and one from an ELDC. You will learn about two diseases, selected from malaria, heart disease or AIDS (Acquired Immune Deficiency Syndrome).

Interaction 5: environmental hazards

This study has a global context and involves the study of a tropical storm, an earthquake and a volcanic eruption.

Top Tip

Be absolutely sure which two interactions you have covered in your course. It is easy to misread the paper or think you can answer one of the other interaction questions. Remember that they each require very specific knowledge.

Your Intermediate 2 Geography exam

Intermediate 2 Geography involves you in completing three units:

- Geography: Physical Environments – British Isles context involving a selection of landscape areas
- Geography: Human Environments – a wider context with studies of detailed examples from EMDCs and ELDCs
- Geography: Environmental Interactions – based on global issues and their management and the interaction between physical and human environments

Your course includes the development of a number of skills relating to OS maps, diagrams and graphs and you will need to be familiar with these.

NABs

Before the main exam in the summer you will not only have sat a prelim but you will also be required to have passed a **National Assessment Bank** test for each of the course units. **NABs** are short unit tests that your teacher will set you when you have covered enough of the topics in each of the units. Normally you get two chances to pass these tests. To gain a unit award you must score **half marks** in each of the three tests you sit in class. NABs are slightly easier than the prelim or the main exam but they will give you some guidance on how you are doing. Your *Success Guide* will help you with the NABs. You must pass them, as well as the main exam, to gain an overall course award.

The Intermediate 2 paper

The Intermediate 2 paper in Geography has **two** sections:

- **Section A**   Question 1 (Physical Environments)
  Question 2 (Human Environments)
- **Section B**   Question 3 (rural land degradation)
  Question 4 (river basin management)
  Question 5 (european environmental inequalities)
  Question 6 (development and health)
  Question 7 (environmental hazards)
- You are required to answer **four** questions from the paper – question 1, question 2 and **two other** questions.
- OS maps may feature in question 1 or question 2.
- Questions 1 and 2 are marked out of 25 and each question in section B is marked out of 15.

Exam technique

It is important that you practise answering the kinds of questions that come up in the exam. You will find examples throughout this book, and also in collections of past papers. Here is a model answer to a question about landform formation.

(i) *Explain how **one** of the following landforms of erosion is formed; you may use diagrams to illustrate your answer:*
headland and bay, stack, arch **(5 marks)**

(ii) *Explain how **one** of the following landforms of deposition is formed; you may use diagrams to illustrate your answer:*
spit, bar, tombolo **(5 marks)**

NB in the following model answers, (1) indicates a point that is worth 1 mark.

Model answer: stack

Stacks are formed when the sea erodes a cliff that juts out to sea (headland). **(1)** It uses erosion processes such as hydraulic action which forces water and compressed air into cracks in the cliff rock and shatters the rock into fragments. **(1)** Corrasion and attrition using these fragments also erode the cliff, particularly in areas of weakness such as faults in the rock strata. **(1)** This opens up caves which become arches when they are eroded right through the headland. **(1)** If the roof of the arch collapses then a pillar of rock, now detached from the cliff is left standing. This is called a stack. **(1)**

Model answer: spit

Spits (bars or tombolos) are formed due to a process called longshore drift. **(1)** This is affected by the direction of the prevailing wind (see diagram) which drives waves towards the shore at an angle. **(1)** The wave washes up the shore until its energy is spent; then it returns to the sea as a backwash at right angles to the slope of the beach. **(1)** Sediment carried by the waves is moved along the beach by this process. If the coast changes direction at a bay or at an estuary, sand deposits build out into the sea as a spit. **(1)** If they build right across the bay they become a sand bar with a lagoon of salt water and salt marshes behind. **(1)** If the spit extends and joins up with an island then it is called a tombolo. **(1)**

The diagram below is worth 1 mark as well.

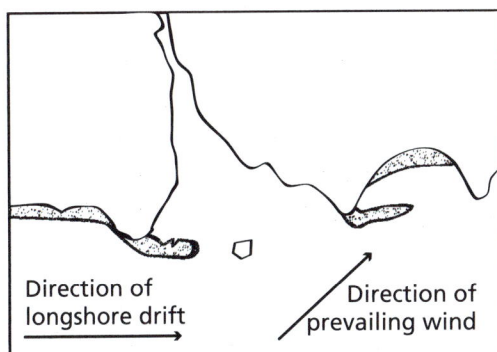

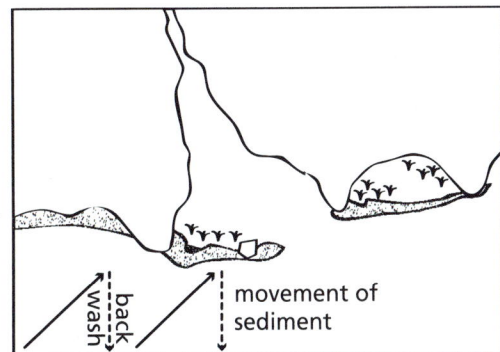

Intermediate 2 Geography
Test and performance analysis

How are you doing in the course?

Performance analysis

Performance analysis is a way of improving your performance over the course by using feedback from tests, written assignments, NABs, prelims and exams. Feedback comes in a number of forms:

- verbal feedback from your teacher
- written feedback on assignments: NABs and exams
- NAB marks
- section marks in tests, NABs, prelims and exams, e.g. limestone, population
- overall marks in tests, prelims and exams

Top Tip
Use test and performance analysis to improve your grade.

Recording information

Set up a file on your computer for recording comments and marks or grades. A spreadsheet is one way of doing this.

ESSAY	MARK	FEEDBACK	ACTION
Urban EMDCs	13/25	Need to be able to use grid references to identify CBD features on OS maps. Need more detail in my answers. Should use the textbook.	Study support grid refs. Read over and take notes from text.
Landscapes	17/25	Good score on glacial erosion. Weaker performance on land use conflicts. Poor on resolving conflicts – not enough case-study detail.	Visit Lake District website. Look up boating on Windermere.

Make good use of comments, marks and advice as the course progresses. Look for improvement as time goes on. Use the systems diagram below as a check on your performance.

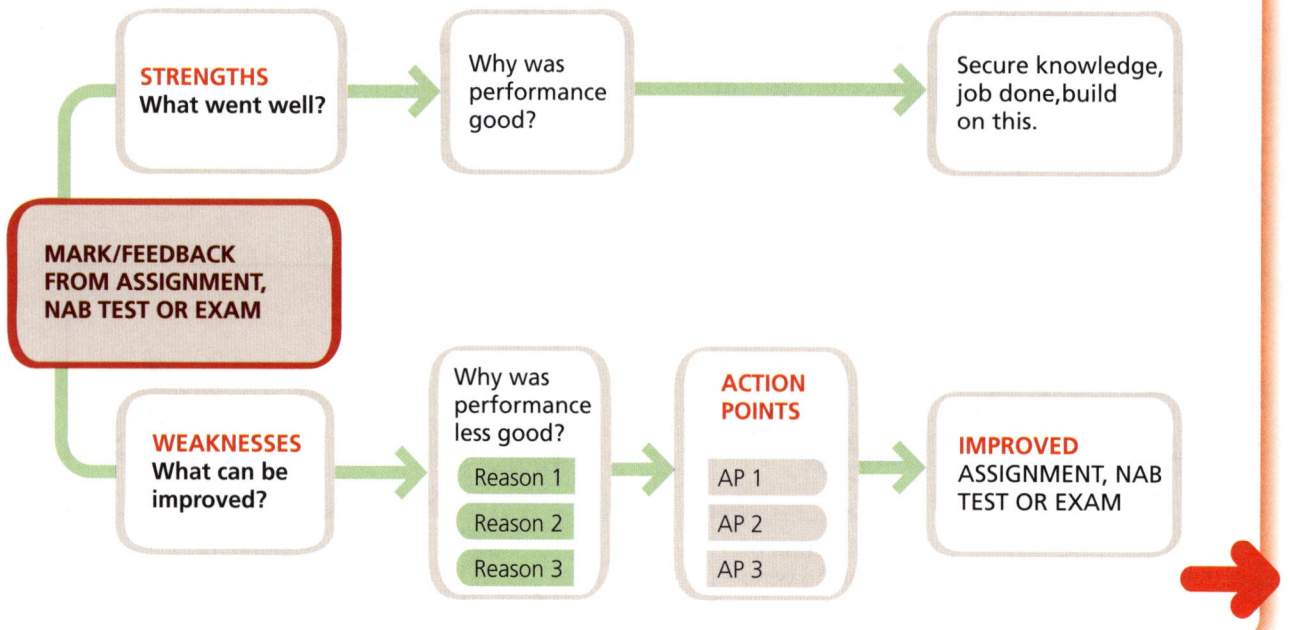

STRENGTHS What went well? → Why was performance good? → Secure knowledge, job done, build on this.

MARK/FEEDBACK FROM ASSIGNMENT, NAB TEST OR EXAM

WEAKNESSES What can be improved? → Why was performance less good? Reason 1, Reason 2, Reason 3 → ACTION POINTS AP 1, AP 2, AP 3 → IMPROVED ASSIGNMENT, NAB TEST OR EXAM

PRELIM	MARK	FEEDBACK	ACTION
Question 1			
a) Map	2/3	Misidentified Yorkshire Dales – limestone.	Learn the base maps in Success Guide.
b) Cross-section	2/3	Got points B and C mixed up.	Take more care identifying features.
			Lay cross-section on map next time.
c) Limestone diagram	6/6	Full marks – know this well.	
d) Environmental impact	3/5	No grid refs, not sure of environmental impact.	Do extra map work at study support.
			Look up textbook and notes.
			Visit Yorkshire Dales website by next week.
e) Land use (i)	2/4	Only covered one land use instead of two as asked for.	Read the questions!!!!!
Land use (ii)	1/4	Ran out of time.	Manage time more effectively. Use bullet points.

Using graphs

You may have to draw and interpret graphs in the exam or NAB tests. Here are some annotated examples.

Example 1 Line graph

- The peak age for giving birth in 1951 (A) was 25 years. The peak age for giving birth in 2001 (B) was just over 30 years.
- In 1951 a peak figure of 225 births per 1000 women was recorded. This had fallen in 2001 to 90 births per 1000 women at the peak.
- Altogether there were fewer births in 2001 compared to 1951.

Births per 1000 women 1951 and 2001, Europe

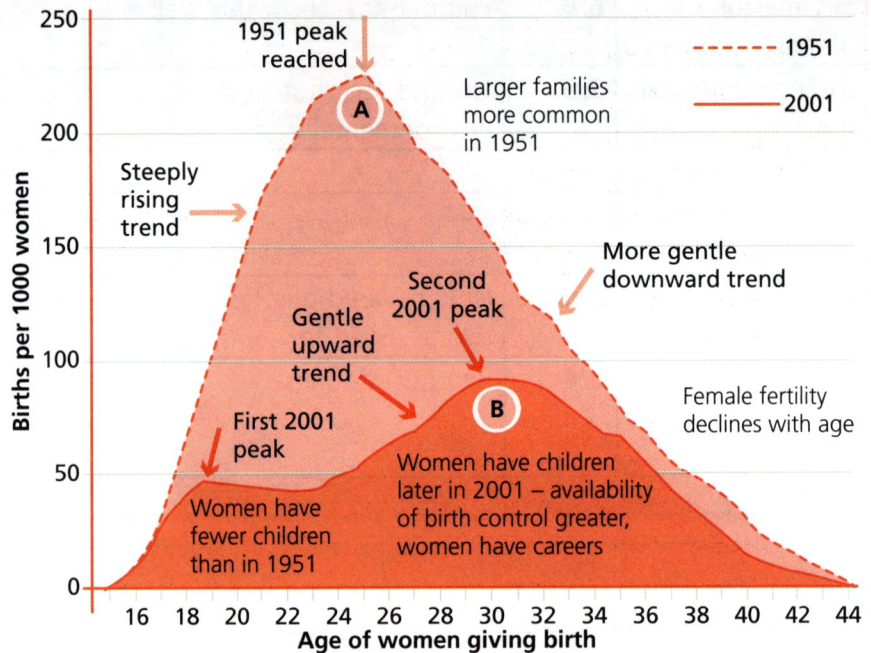

1951 peak reached

Larger families more common in 1951

Steeply rising trend

More gentle downward trend

Second 2001 peak

Gentle upward trend

First 2001 peak

Female fertility declines with age

Women have children later in 2001 – availability of birth control greater, women have careers

Women have fewer children than in 1951

- - - - 1951
——— 2001

Births per 1000 women

Age of women giving birth

Example 2 Climate graph

Compare highest temperature with rainfall total – what do you see?

Compare lowest rainfall with temperature – what do you notice?

What figures can you quote for rainfall and temperature? Pick out highs and lows.

Climate graph, Grootfontein

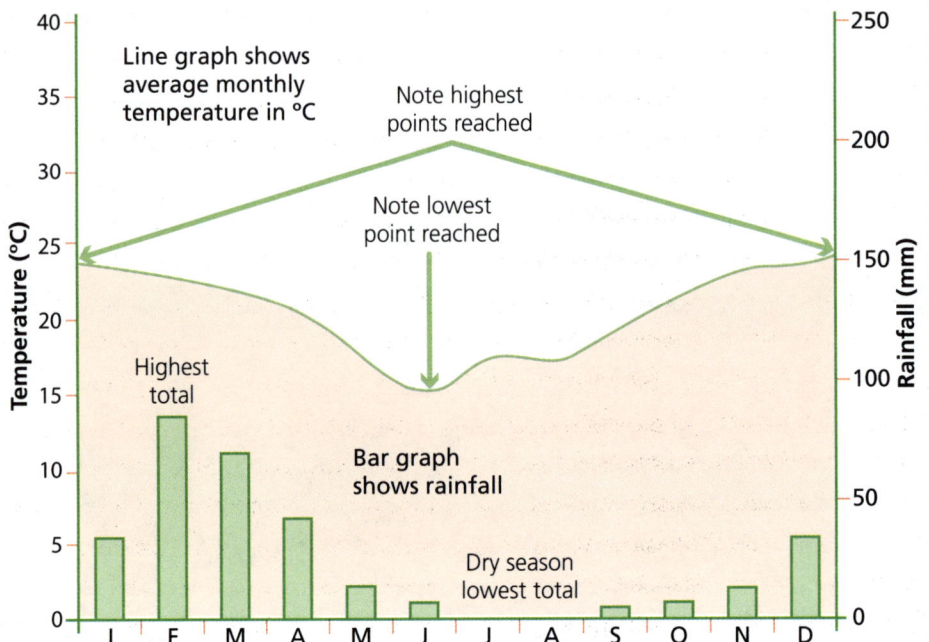

Line graph shows average monthly temperature in °C

Note highest points reached

Note lowest point reached

Highest total

Bar graph shows rainfall

Dry season lowest total

Temperature (°C)

Rainfall (mm)

J F M A M J J A S O N D

Example 3 Scatter graph

Scatter graphs show relationships between sets of data. You should be able to draw a scatter graph and comment on what it shows.

As GNP gets higher so does the total number of calories consumed per day.

As people become more wealthy they can spend more on food.

Although wealth can increase more, there comes a point where calorie intake is unlikely to get higher.

GNP ($) versus calories per day for selected countries

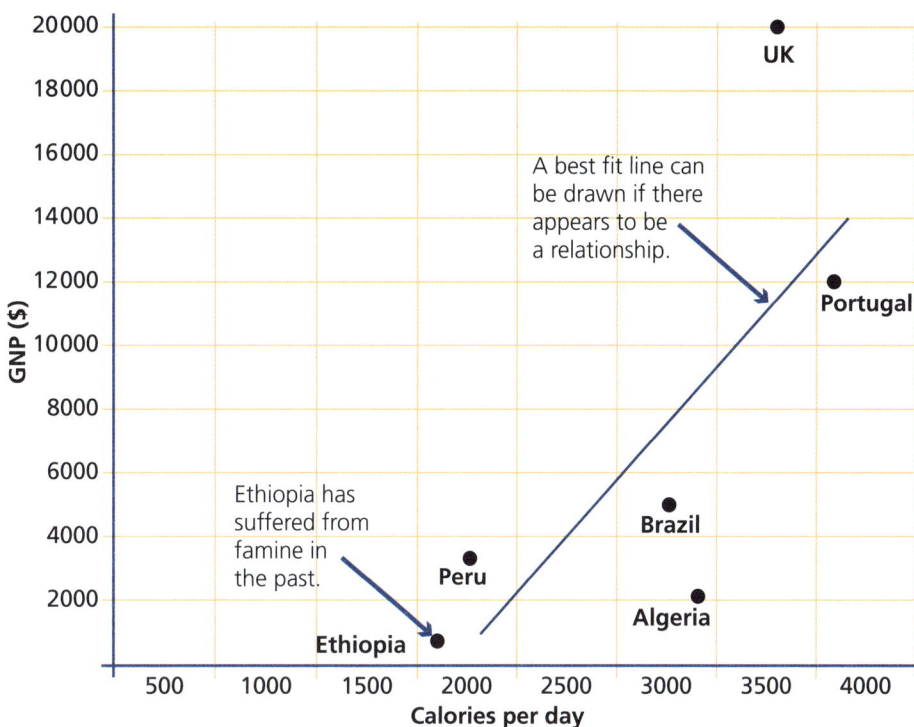

A best fit line can be drawn if there appears to be a relationship.

Ethiopia has suffered from famine in the past.

Example 4 Divided bar graph

Quote figures from different years in your answer. For example, 72% rural in 1975 but 52% rural (projected) in 2015.

Note the increasing percentages and growing proportions.

Add cities and other urban together for total urban (48%)

Compare this with 28% in 1975.

Note the decline in rural population as people move to the cities.

Population figures

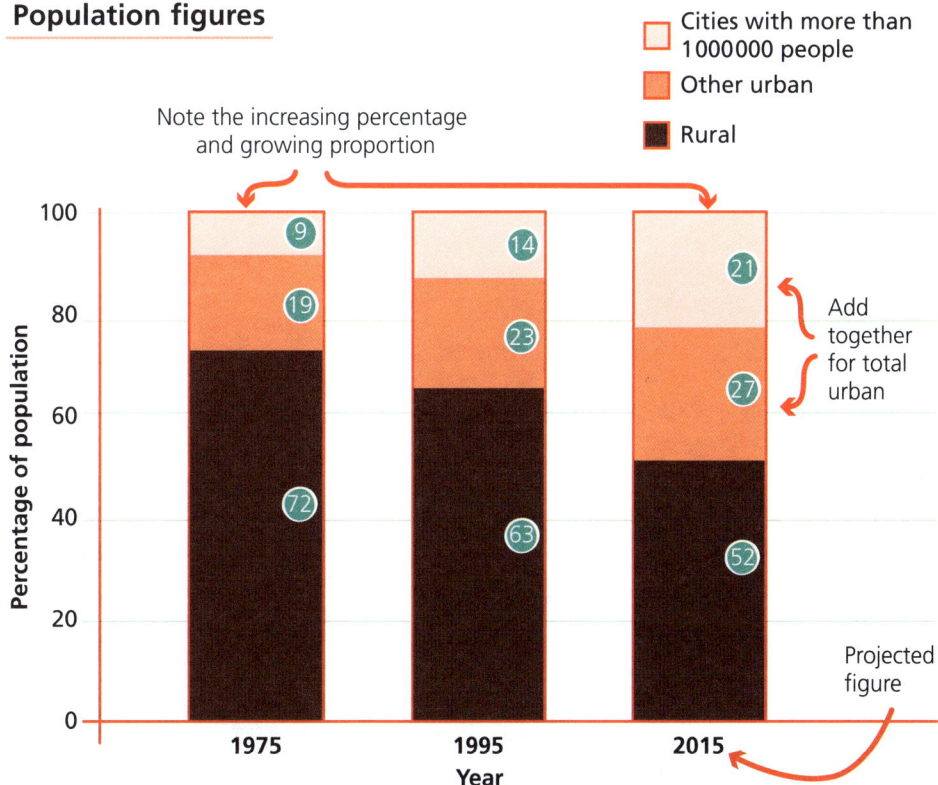

Cities with more than 1000000 people

Other urban

Rural

Note the increasing percentage and growing proportion

Add together for total urban

Projected figure

Glaciated landscapes 1

Glaciation and the effects of the ice age are a key part of the course. You will study one of the glaciated mountain areas such as the Cairngorms, Loch Lomond and the Trossachs, the Lake District, Snowdonia or the Brecon Beacons.

This question may involve the use of an **Ordnance Survey (OS) map** so you should be able to recognise typical glacial features and also be able to use a 6 figure grid reference to identify them on a map. Can you spot the following features on an OS map? *Corrie, tarn/corrie loch, pyramidal peak, arête, U-shaped valley, misfit stream, truncated spur, hanging valley, ribbon lake.*

In addition to identifying the range of glacial features on a map or diagram, you may be asked to explain the formation of features such as a corrie or a U-shaped valley.

See larger, labelled map on www.leckieandleckie.co.uk.

How do corries form?

To answer this question successfully you will need to use the following **bullet words**: *rotational slip*, *plucking* and *abrasion*. By using them appropriately in sentences you should be able to score at least 3 marks.

Top Tip
Bullet words are geographical words that are likely to score a mark in an exam answer. Try to learn as many as you can.

Pyramidal peak, Cairngorms

Corries

Corries are formed when snow collects in north facing hollows, where snow is less likely to melt. Over time it becomes glacier ice. The ice wraps itself around the bedrock below it. The ice begins to move out of the hollows due to gravity, using a process called **rotational slip**. This tears rocks and boulders away from the ground in a process called **plucking**. Loose rocks, boulders and stones embedded in the ice of the glacier grind the landscape away like sandpaper in a process called **abrasion**. Over time the hollow becomes over-deepened and when the ice melts at the end of the ice age the steep-sided armchair-shaped corrie is left behind on the mountainside. A small lake called a tarn may form in the bottom of the corrie.

Use a simple diagram like the one below to help you explain how the corrie is formed. You should try to give examples of corries you have studied in your course to really enhance your answer, e.g. **Lake District** – *Red Tarn*, **Cairngorms** – *Coire an Lochan*, **Snowdonia** – *Cwm Idwal*.

At the start of the ice age

Ice collects in pre-existing hollows high on the mountain-side, especially on north-facing slopes.

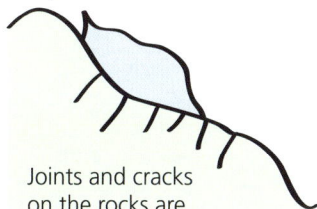

Joints and cracks on the rocks are weaknesses

During the ice age

A glacier has formed.

It moves due to rotational slip caused by gravity.

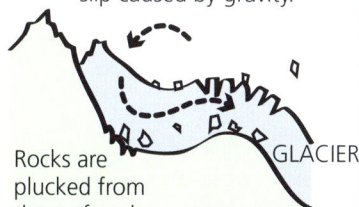

Rocks are plucked from the surface by the ice as it moves.

Rocks erode the landscape by scraping (abrasion).

GLACIER

After the ice age

Corrie and tarn

Pyramidal peak

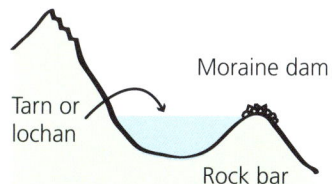

Moraine dam

Tarn or lochan

Rock bar

Overdeepened armchair-shaped hollow (corrie)

You should learn how to draw simple annotated diagrams like these to answer the question 'with the aid of a diagram or diagrams, explain how a corrie is formed'.

For another illustration of the formation of corries, please visit www.leckieandleckie.co.uk.

Glaciated landscapes 2

How are U-shaped valleys formed?

Once again, the bullet words **plucking** and **abrasion** have to be used to explain the process of erosion. A series of three line diagrams – before, during and after the ice age – will illustrate your answer effectively (see below).

Before the ice age
Before the ice age, rivers cut v-shaped valleys.

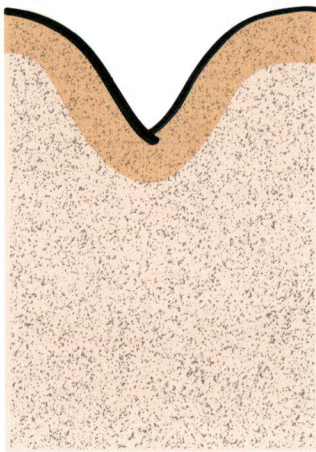

During the ice age
During the ice age, a glacier erodes the valley.

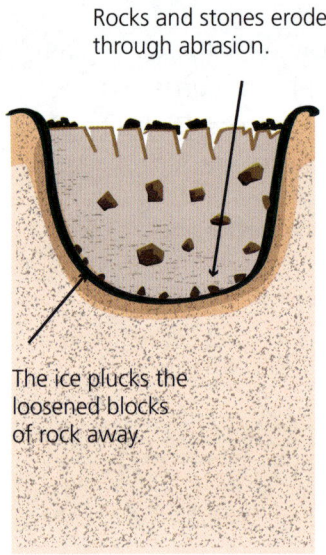

Rocks and stones erode through abrasion.

The ice plucks the loosened blocks of rock away.

After the ice age

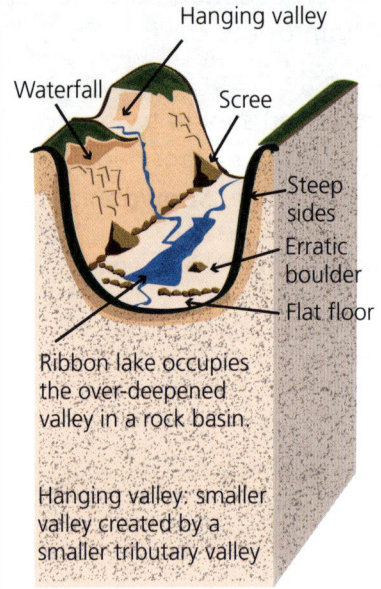

Hanging valley

Waterfall

Scree

Steep sides

Erratic boulder

Flat floor

Ribbon lake occupies the over-deepened valley in a rock basin.

Hanging valley: smaller valley created by a smaller tributary valley

Before the ice age, V-shaped valleys were formed by rivers. (See diagram 1: before the ice age.) During the ice age, glaciers eroded these valleys using plucking and abrasion. (See diagram 2: during the ice age.) At the end of the ice age, the ice melted and left behind a steep-sided flat floored U-shaped valley. (See diagram 3: after the ice age.)

Examples of U-shaped valleys include: **Lake District** – *Langdale*, **Cairngorms** – *Glen Avon*, **Snowdonia** – *Nant Ffrancon Valley*.

U-shaped valley Glen Avon

Hanging valleys

Smaller tributary glaciers will have joined the main glacier. These do not erode the landscape as deeply, and they leave behind hanging valleys perched high above the main valley floor. Waterfalls may be found coming down the steep slope created between the main valley and its tributary.

Arêtes and pyramidal peaks

These are formed when several corries are cut back to back and eat into the mountainside from different directions. This creates the pyramidal-shaped peak and the knife edged ridges that lead up to its summit, called arêtes. Case-study examples will add weight to your answer.

Top Tip
Bullet words for glaciation answers are *plucking, abrasion* and *rotational slip*. Be sure to use them and explain their meaning. Use simple annotated line diagrams and examples to add value to your answers.

Quick Test

1. Explain how plucking works.

2. Explain how abrasion works.

3. Complete the table below by listing some the main glacial landscape features found in a mountain area you have studied, such as the Lake District.

Glacial feature	Lake District example
U-shaped valley	Langdale

Answers 1. Plucking is the tearing action of a glacier on bedrock. **2.** Abrasion is the sandpaper effect as a glacier grinds the rock beneath it.

Limestone landscapes

Limestone is a common rock found in many parts of the British Isles (see the map of **Upland Scenery in the British Isles** on page 12 and on www.leckieandleckie.co.uk). What makes limestone, and in particular carboniferous limestone, special is the fact that it is soluble in rainwater. This produces a whole range of features which can be found in limestone landscapes.

Bedding plane

Joint

You will be expected to be able to explain the formation of a number of limestone features from above and below ground. You will also have studied an area of limestone scenery such as the Yorkshire Dales or the Peak District National Park.

Clints and grykes

Limestone on OS maps and diagrams

You should be able to spot the following limestone features on OS maps like the one in this section and on the diagrams provided: **limestone pavement, stalagmites and stalactites, limestone gorge, swallow holes and potholes, cave or cavern, clint, gryke, scree slopes, intermittent drainage**.

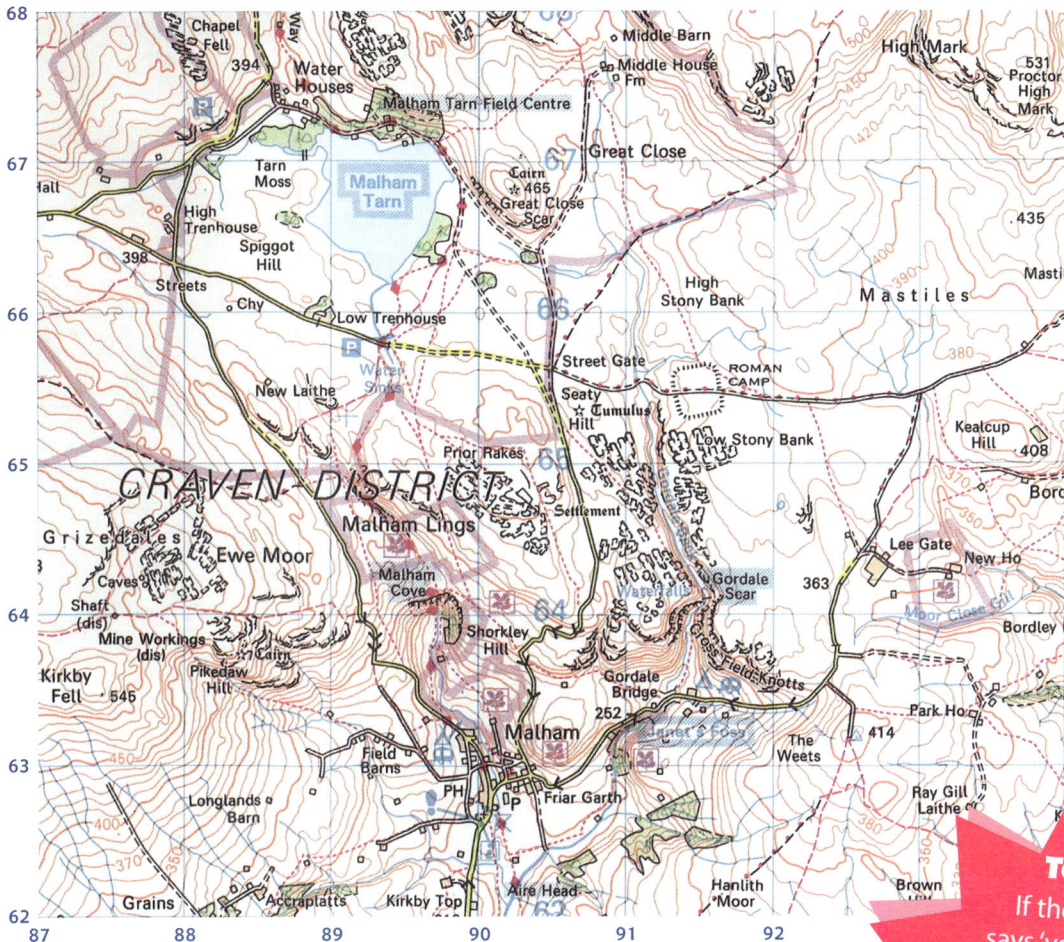

Top Tip
If the question says 'you may use a diagram(s)' **you should think about** using a diagram(s) to help your explanation. Diagrams score marks!

Quick Test

Study the Ordnance Survey map extract showing part of the Yorkshire Dales National Park.

(i) Match the following grid references to the list of features of upland limestone
Grid references: 876643   893658   900647   914640
Features: swallow hole, caves, gorge, limestone pavement

(ii) Select one of the features from the list above and explain how it was formed. You may use diagrams if you wish.

Answers (i) 876643 – caves; 893658 – swallow hole; 900647 – limestone pavement; 914640 – gorge. **(ii)** Answers should include ideas such as acidic rainwater (carbonic acid) dissolving limestone beds and joints to open them up. Streams disappear down opened joints. Words like clints and grykes should be included. Waterfalls could involve the roof of a cave collapsing.

Limestone landscapes and limestone features

You need to be able to recognise a range of limestone features on a diagram.

ABOVE GROUND: clint, gryke, limestone pavement, swallow hole, pot hole, sink hole, disappearing stream, gorge.

BELOW GROUND: cavern, stalagmite, stalactite.

You should be able to spot these features on model landscape diagrams, as well as on OS maps, where required.

Top Tip
Bullet words that will score points in limestone answers are **joints, carbonic acid, permeable, impermeable, soluble, calcium carbonate, calcite.**

Block diagram showing limestone features

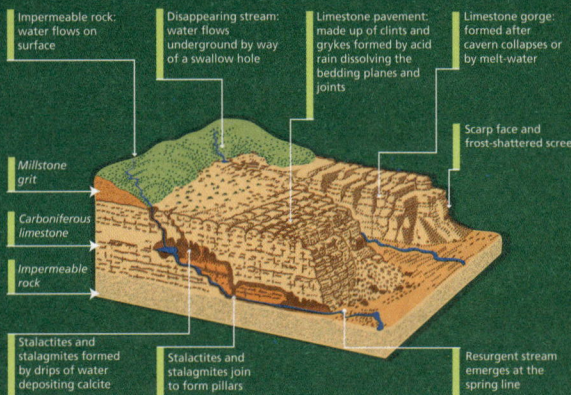

Impermeable rock: water flows on surface

Disappearing stream: water flows underground by way of a swallow hole

Limestone pavement: made up of clints and grykes formed by acid rain dissolving the bedding planes and joints

Limestone gorge: formed after cavern collapses or by melt-water

Millstone grit

Carboniferous limestone

Impermeable rock

Scarp face and frost-shattered scree

Stalactites and stalagmites formed by drips of water depositing calcite

Stalactites and stalagmites join to form pillars

Resurgent stream emerges at the spring line

See larger version of this diagram on www.leckieandleckie.co.uk.

Limestone pavement

Limestone is made up of the shells and dead bodies of sea life. It was laid down in beds. Each bed of limestone is separated from others by horizontal bedding planes. As the limestone mass dried out or as a consequence of earth movements, vertical cracks formed called joints.

Falling rain dissolves carbon dioxide in the atmosphere which turns it into weak carbonic acid. This dissolves limestone, especially where the landscape was stripped bare of soil by glaciers that left the soluble rock open to attack. Joints and bedding planes are especially under attack and are enlarged over time.

Chemical weathering and the formation of limestone pavements

Limestone pavement with clints and grykes at Malham Cove

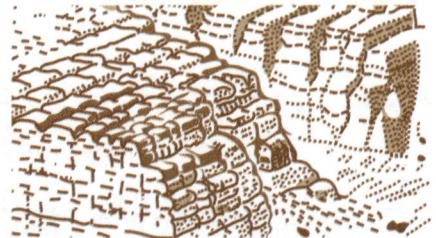

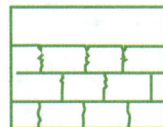

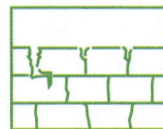

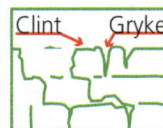

1. Limestone has horizontal cracks called bedding planes and vertical cracks called joints.

2. Acid rain-water dissolves the limestone along the bedding planes and joints.

Clint Gryke

3. Limestone pavements form.

The surface joints are dissolved to form crevices called **grykes** with upstanding blocks of limestone in between called **clints**. Large areas of clints and grykes can be found on the limestone uplands and are called **limestone pavements** because of their block structure.

Malham Pavements

Top Tip

Learn the landscape features you need in your answers by studying the diagrams on p18–19 or in your notes. Practise drawing and labelling them.

Other limestone features

Dissolution of limestone in this way also creates other limestone features. Acid rainwater forms streams which open up joints and bedding planes to form **swallow holes** or water sinks (**sink holes**) where streams disappear underground leaving dry valleys on the surface. Joints and bedding planes can be opened up beneath the surface and eroded into massive **caverns** and connecting passages as water flows underground.

Underground streams eventually meet impermeable rock layers beneath the limestone, such as clay, and reappear on the surface as a **resurgent stream**. These often resurface at the foot of a limestone **scarp** or **scar** (steep almost vertical rock face).

Top Tip

STALA**C**TITE – **C** FOR CEILING STALA**G**MITE – **G** FOR GROUND

Underground features

Stalagmites and stalactites are formed in caves and caverns from the water dripping from the ceiling of the cave. This water is charged with calcium carbonate in solution. As the water drips from the ceiling of the cave it leaves behind a tiny deposit of calcium carbonate mineral called calcite. This builds up like a stone icicle hanging from the roof of the cave and is called a **stalactite**. The drips fall to the ground below where calcite is again deposited to form a **stalagmite** which grows upwards towards the roof. If a stalactite and stalagmite meet and join together they form a limestone pillar.

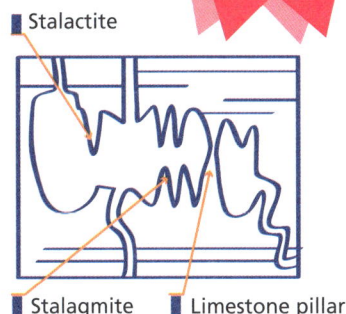

■ Stalactite

■ Stalagmite   ■ Limestone pillar

Quick Test

1. Why does rainwater weather limestone?
2. How do clints and grykes form?
3. What would limestone pavement look like on an OS map?
4. How do swallow holes form?
5. How are stalactites and stalagmites created?

Answers **1.** Because it has formed a weak acid by dissolving carbon dioxide in the atmosphere. This dissolves limestone. **2.** Acidic water (see above) picks out the limestone joints and opens them up to form fissures-(grykes) and blocks (clints). **3.** Areas of bare rock drawn in black. **4.** By a stream opening up a joint and then flowing down it underground. **5.** Drips from the roof of a cave leave behind calcite deposits in an icicle shape (stalactite). Splashes onto the floor of a cave leave a similar upward growing deposit (stalagmite).

Coastal landscapes

In this section of the paper you will be expected to know how coastal landscapes are formed by the sea interacting with the local geology. You should be able to identify and locate areas of coastal scenery on the map of the British Isles. In addition, you should be able to identify and explain the formation of a number of features of coastal erosion and deposition.

N. W. Scotland
(rugged cliffs, sandy bays, depositional features, Old Man of Stoer stack)

Antrim
(Giant's Causeway, rugged cliffs, deposition of sand)

Connemara
(rugged cliffs, sand dunes, spits and bars)

Pembrokeshire
(National Park, rugged cliffs, stacks, arches, spits and bars)

S. W. England
(rugged cliff scenery)

N. E. Scotland
(rugged cliff scenery, sand dunes, spits and bars)

Northumberland
(rugged cliffs, sand dunes, spits and bars)

Norfolk
(wetlands, low cliffs, sand and depositional features)

S. E. England
(rugged chalk cliffs, spits and bars)

Dorset
(Old Harry stack rocks, Durdle Door Arch, Lulworth Cove, Chesil beach, spits and bars)

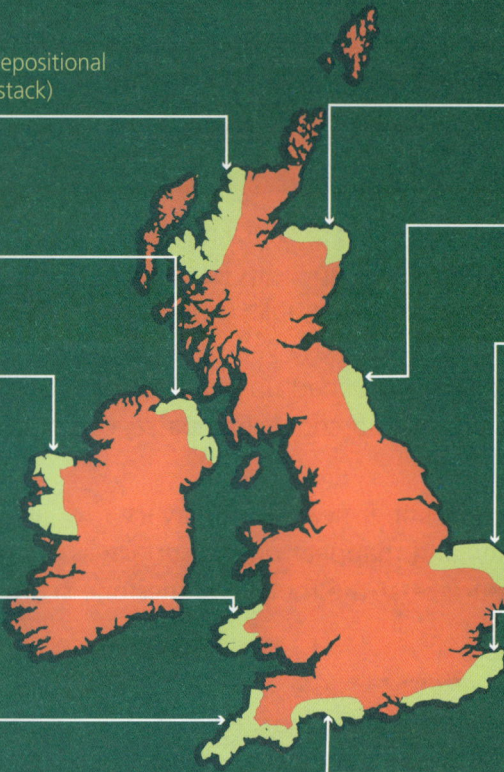

Coastal erosion and deposition involves three processes: **erosion** of the coast, **transportation** of sediment and **deposition** of sediment.

Erosion processes

Erosion by the sea works in a similar way to erosion by rivers (see later in the book) and breaks the landscape down in much the same way. You should be able to explain how the sea erodes the coast using some of the following processes:

- **Hydraulic action:** the force of the waves pushes air and water into cracks in the bedrock exploiting the weaknesses in the natural cracks and crevices. This high pressure air and water forced into cracks widens them and the rock breaks up.

- **Corrasion:** this occurs when large and small fragments of rock such as pebbles and boulders rub the surface of the sea bed, grinding it away.

- **Attrition:** this happens when rock fragments carried by the waves collide and break up into smaller and smaller fragments.

Top Tip
Knowing about the way in which rivers erode the landscape helps you answer the coastal erosion question too. Learn these processes well and kill two birds with one stone.

Transportation processes

Like rivers, waves on the seashore carry sediment (stones, sand and silt) which erodes the cliffs or is deposited where the sea moves less forcefully and tidal currents are less strong. Sediment moves along the coast by rolling along (**traction**), by bouncing along (**saltation**) or by floating along (**suspension**). Sediment in the form of sand is also transported along the beaches by the wind in much the same way.

You should be able to identify and label a range of coastal erosion features. The diagrams below will help you.

Top Tip
Bullet words for coastal erosion are **hydraulic action, corrasion** and **attrition**.

The formation of cliff scenery

The start of the process.
Picture 1 shows a cliff coastline with a headland that runs out to the sea. The sea is able to erode the cliffs at high tides. It attacks the cracks between the beds of rock and the faults which are easy to wear away. Materials broken off the cliffs go to make a beach in the nearby bay. A cave has formed at B where a fault cuts the rock of the cliffs.

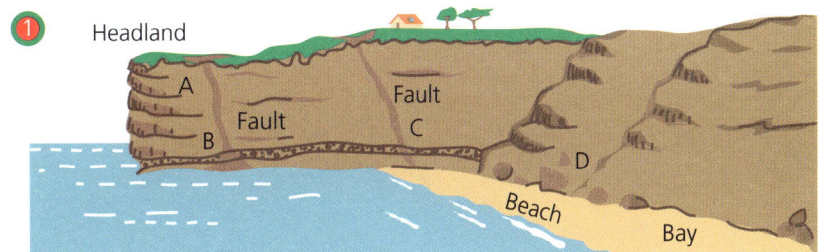

Many years later
Picture 2 shows how the sea has been at work. The point of headland A is still attached but an arch has formed at B where the sea has worn through the headland. Another cave is forming at the fault at C. A crack at D is opening up. During storms, the sea explodes up into the roof at B and has cut a blowhole up to the top of the cliff. This is called a gloop.

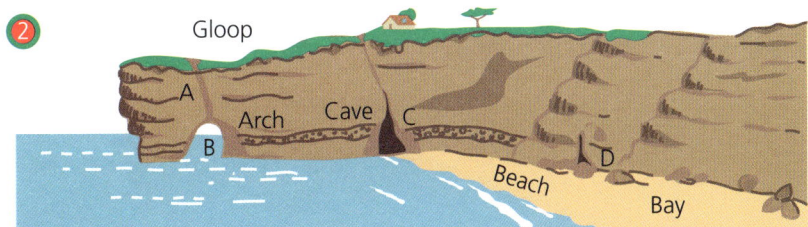

Many years later still
In picture 3, the arch at B collapsed some years ago, turning A into a stack. The cave at C has become an arch and D is now a cave. At E, there has been a landslip where the sea has undermined the cliff. People in the house are trying to sell up but are not having much success!

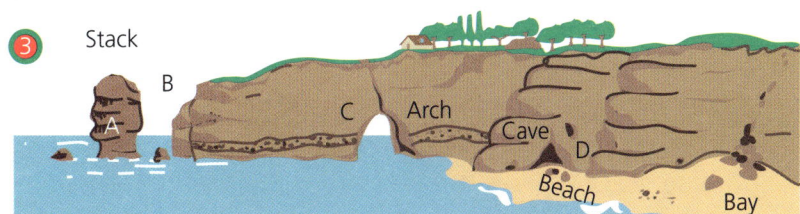

The formation of caves, arches and stacks

Stacks are formed when the sea erodes a cliff that juts out to sea (**headland**). It uses **hydraulic action** which forces water and compressed air into cracks in the cliff and shatters the cliff rock into fragments. **Corrasion** and **attrition,** using these fragments, also erode the cliff, particularly in the weaker parts of the rock such as faults and bedding planes. This opens up caves which become arches when they are eroded right through the headland. If the roof of the arch collapses then a pillar of rock, now detached from the cliff, is left standing. This is called a stack.

Coastal landscapes: deposition

The formation of spits, bars and tombolos

Spits, bars and tombolos are formed due to a process called longshore drift. This is affected by the direction of the prevailing wind (see diagram) which drives waves towards the shore at an angle. The wave washes up the shore until its energy is spent, then it returns to the sea as a backwash at right angles to the slope of the beach. Sediment carried by the waves is moved along the beach by this process. If the coast changes direction at a bay or an estuary, sand deposits build out into the sea as a spit. If the deposits build right across the bay they become a sand bar with a lagoon of salt water and salt marshes behind. If the spit extends and joins up with an island then it is called a tombolo.

Top Tip
Bullet words for coastal deposition are **longshore drift**, **swash, backwash** and **prevailing wind**.

The formation of spits, bars and tombolos

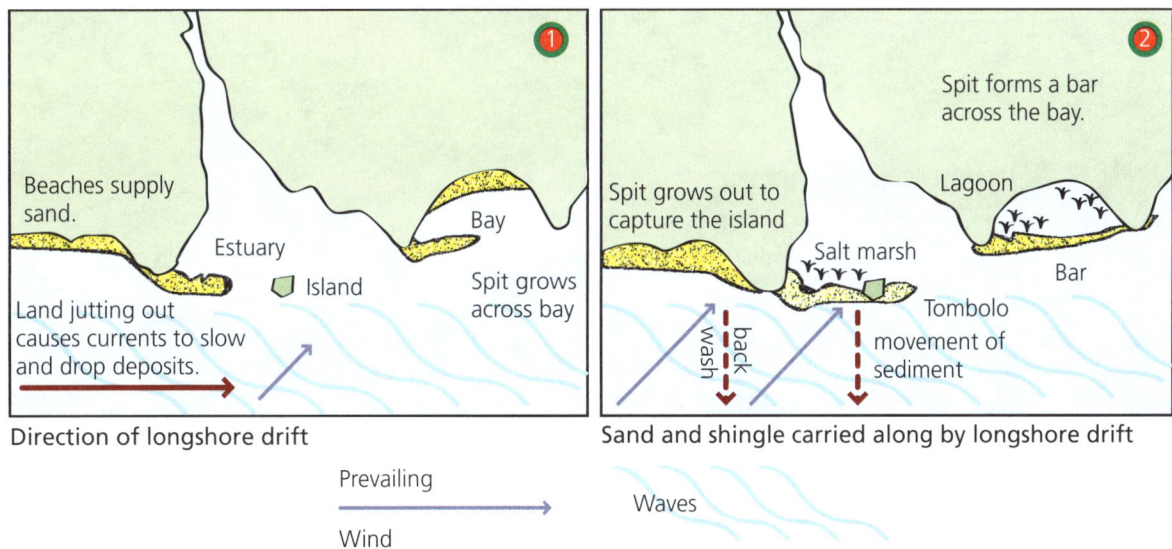

Quick Test

1. What are the main processes of erosion used by the sea to erode the land?
2. How is an arch formed?
3. What is longshore drift?
4. How do tombolos form?

Answers 1. Hydraulic action, corrasion, attrition. **2.** The sea picks out weaknesses in a headland such as a fault line and creates a cave which is eroded right through to form an arch. **3.** The movement of sediment along a beach, determined by the direction of the prevailing wind. **4.** Longshore drift extends a spit out to an island creating a natural causeway.

River landscapes

In this section of the paper you will be expected to know about rivers and their valleys. You should also be prepared to draw diagrams to help you explain how river features such as waterfalls and meanders are formed. You will also be expected to know and identify the rivers shown on the reference map below.

Main rivers of the British Isles

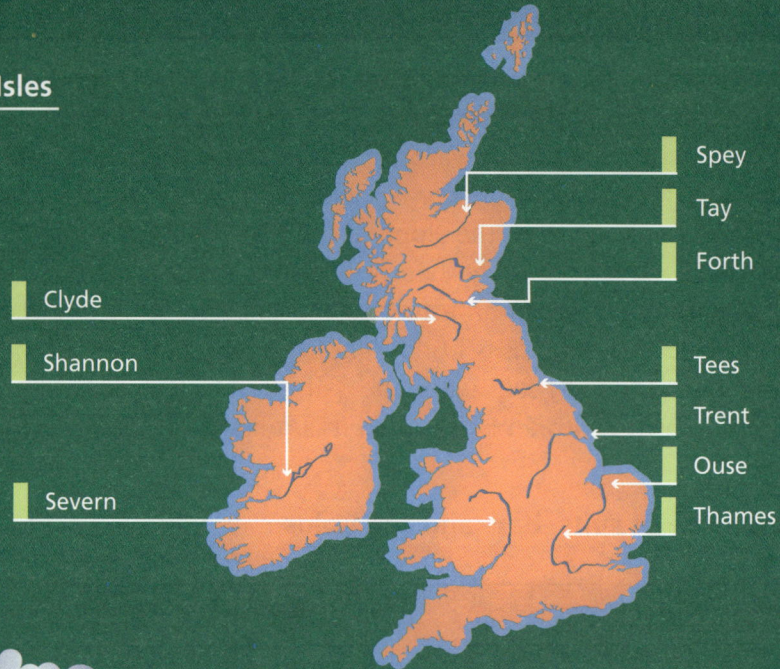

Spey

Tay

Forth

Clyde

Shannon

Tees

Trent

Ouse

Severn

Thames

Profile of a river's course

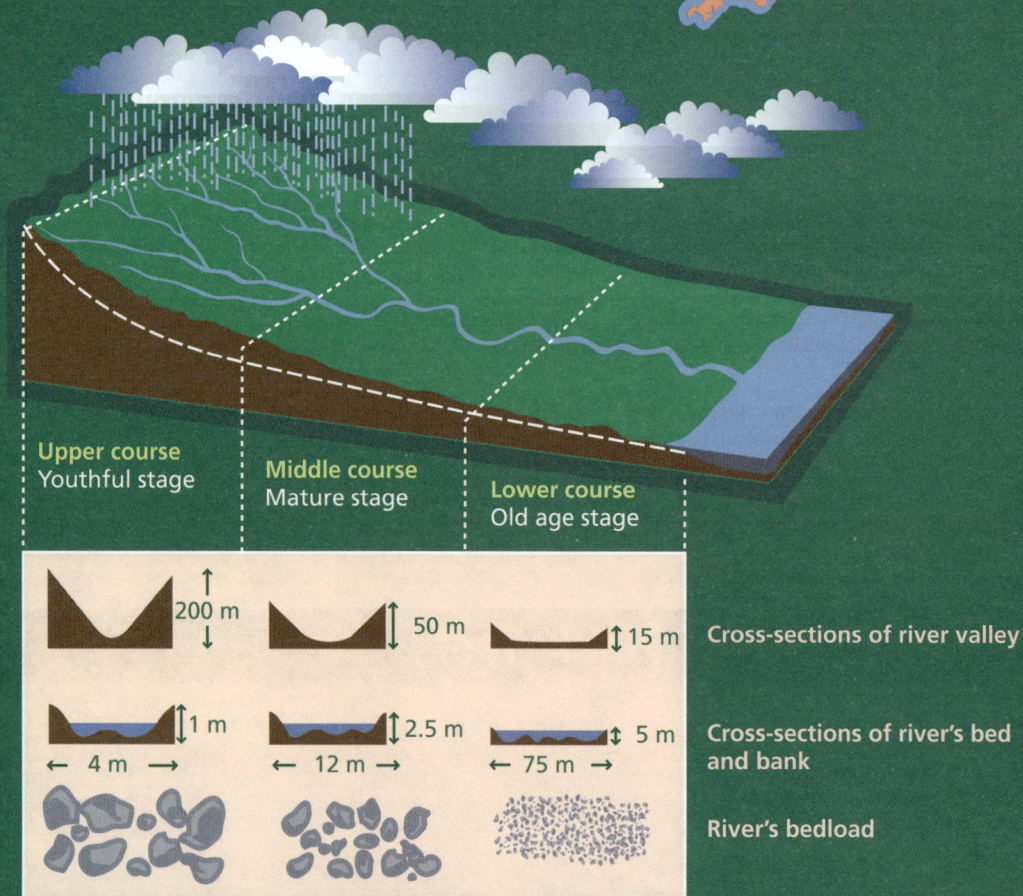

Upper course
Youthful stage

Middle course
Mature stage

Lower course
Old age stage

200 m

50 m

15 m

Cross-sections of river valley

1 m

2.5 m

5 m

← 4 m →

← 12 m →

← 75 m →

Cross-sections of river's bed and bank

River's bedload

Rivers have three stages of development. Near the river's source in the mountains is the **youthful stage**; lower downstream, in the middle of the river's course, is the **mature stage** and at the end of its journey to the sea the river goes into its **old age stage**. The table below summarises river and river stage terms that might be used interchangeably, and associated river features.

River stage	River course	River landscape	River features
1. Youth	Upper course	Mountain stage	V-shaped valleys, waterfalls
2. Maturity	Middle course	Valley stage	meanders, braiding
3. Old age	Lower course	Plain stage	oxbow lake, levee, flood plain

As with coastal erosion and deposition, rivers involve three processes: **erosion** of the landscape, **transportation** of sediment and **deposition** of sediment.

Erosion processes

Erosion by rivers breaks the landscape down. You should be able to explain how rivers erode their valleys using some of the following processes.

- **Hydraulic action** where the river pushes air and water into cracks in the river bed and the rock breaks up.
- **Corrasion** occurs when large and small fragments of rock such as pebbles and boulders rub the surface of the river bed, grinding it away.
- **Attrition** happens when rock fragments carried by the river collide and break up into smaller and smaller fragments.
- **Corrosion and solution** happen when the river water dissolves the bedrock, for example, acid rainwater will dissolve limestone.

Transportation and deposition processes

Rivers carry the eroded materials along and may deposit them later. (See meanders and levees on pages 28 and 29.)

Quick Test

1. How do rivers erode the landscape?
2. What is hydraulic action?
3. What is attrition?
4. What is solution?

Answers 1. By means of hydraulic action, attrition, corrasion, corrosion and solution. **2.** When the river pushes compressed air into cracks and crevices causing erosion. **3.** When fragments of sediment collide and are broken into smaller fragments. **4.** When water dissolves rocks like limestone.

The formation of river features

You should be able to recognise river landscape features on diagrams like the one on page 27. You will also be expected to explain how some of these features were formed, most typically either a waterfall or a meander and oxbow lake. See the exam-style question in the Quick Test.

Top Tip

Draw large simple sketch diagrams of physical landscape features, label them and hang them up in obvious places as you revise. Then you will be able to study them at a glance without having to open your books or notes.

Formation of waterfalls

Waterfalls are formed when a river flows over alternating beds of hard and soft rock. Erosion takes place using **hydraulic action**, where air and water are forced into the cracks in the bedrock, or **corrasion**, where the river grinds away at the bedrock using its load of sand and gravel. This erodes the weaker rock more than the harder rock above (see diagram). Erosion undermines the hard rock on top until it cannot be supported and collapses into the stream. In this way the river cuts backwards into the landscape forming a waterfall and steep sided gorge.

Undercut hard rock collapses and the waterfall retreats upstream.

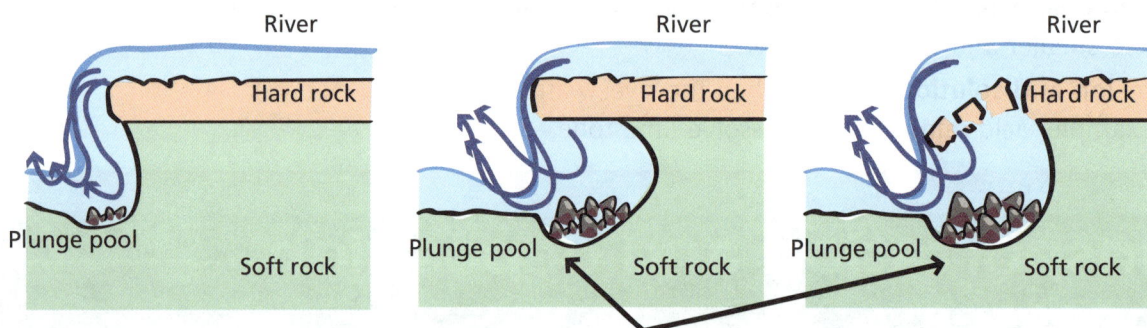

Undercutting takes place as the river erodes the soft rock by hydraulic action and abrasion.

Formation of meanders

Rivers do not flow in a straight line. Contact between the river water and the river's sides and bed make the water turbulent. Turbulent flow causes the water in the river to flow from side to side. This is called the river meandering. The speed of flow is greater in a meander on the outside of the bend so erosion takes place here (see diagram). Erosion takes place using **hydraulic action** where air and water is forced into the cracks in the bedrock or **corrasion** where the river grinds away at the bedrock. On the inside of the bend the flow rate is slower so the river deposits here. Over time erosion of the outside bends into the neck of the **meander** sees the space in between eroded away more and more until the river breaks through to form a new course. The old river course is abandoned and an **oxbow lake** is left behind.

Formation of a meander and an oxbow lake

1. River meanders. Erosion on the outside of the bends leads to…

2. … the meander becoming incised.

3. In time, floodwater breaks through the incised neck.

4. The river abandons its old course, leaving the oxbow lake behind.

Other river processes

By using the erosion processes above it is possible to explain the formation of V-shaped river valleys.

Braiding takes place where the river current is slow and sand and gravel is deposited by the river which causes the river to break up into several channels called braids. By using the transportation and erosion processes given above you will be able to explain this feature.

Levees are found in the lower course where the river has created a low lying flood plain. As the river bursts its banks its flow slows down as it leaves its channel. This leaves a deposit of sediment which over time builds up a raised bank alongside the river called a levee. Levees may prevent the river from flooding if people build them higher.

Rivers on OS maps

You should be able to identify river features on an OS map and explain how they were formed. The diagrams below will help you spot the patterns associated with some of the main river features.

Main river features on OS maps

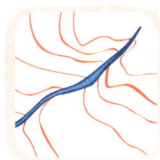

V-shaped river valley

Meander and oxbow lake

Levees to prevent flooding

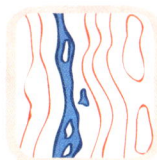

Braided stream

Waterfall and gorge

Quick Test

1. How does the river undermine the waterfall?
2. What is an oxbow lake?
3. How are levees formed?

Exam-style questions

(i) Explain the formation of a waterfall. You may use diagrams to illustrate your answer. **(4)**
Or
(ii) Explain the formation of a meander. You may use diagrams to illustrate your answer. **(4)**

Answers 1. The swirling action below the waterfall undercuts the rock face behind the waterfall. **2.** It is a meander that has been abandoned by the river after it breaks through the meander neck. **3.** Levees are formed by a river bursting its banks and leaving behind sediment on the river's edge.

Land use in mountain environments

It is important not only to know how the landscape was formed, but also to know how people interact with and use the landscape. This is often tested in the context of specific National Parks where a particular scenery type dominates, such as glaciation in the Lake District or Snowdonia, or carboniferous limestone scenery (karst) in the Yorkshire Dales or the Peak District.

You will need to know about land use in each of the landscape areas: glaciated mountains, limestone uplands and coastal areas. Some of the issues involved are shown in the diagram below and the illustration on page 35, **Mountain land use**.

National Park land use model

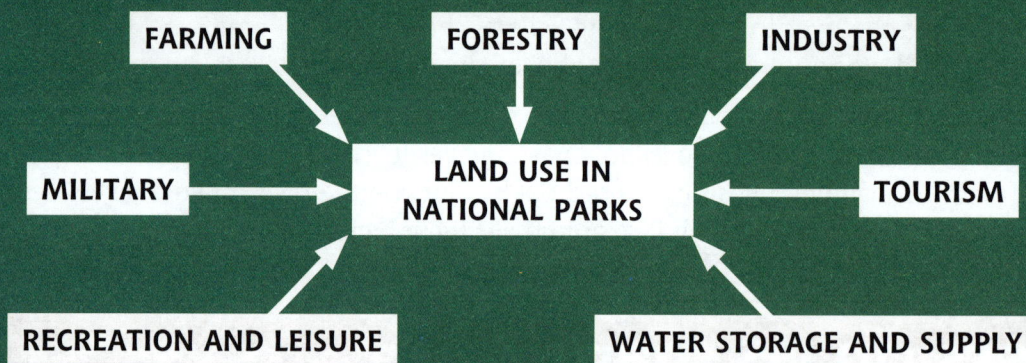

FARMING → LAND USE IN NATIONAL PARKS

FORESTRY → LAND USE IN NATIONAL PARKS

INDUSTRY → LAND USE IN NATIONAL PARKS

MILITARY → LAND USE IN NATIONAL PARKS

TOURISM → LAND USE IN NATIONAL PARKS

RECREATION AND LEISURE → LAND USE IN NATIONAL PARKS

WATER STORAGE AND SUPPLY → LAND USE IN NATIONAL PARKS

Types of land use in mountain environments

Farming

Farming is a dominant land use in glaciated and limestone upland areas. However, steep slopes make using modern farm machinery difficult. Also, upland climates are often too cold to allow the growing of crops for cash and these areas have high rainfall and poor quality soils which limit farming opportunities. Additionally, poor roads and weather conditions make getting to markets difficult. Hill sheep and hill cattle farming dominate where farmers use the hillsides for grazing and valley bottoms with better soils and weather conditions for growing fodder crops.

Forestry

Land often unsuitable for farming can be used for forestry as conifers in particular can survive in the harsh mountain conditions. Trees will grow on steep slopes and in poorer soils. They are suited to the harsh weather of the mountains. Many jobs are created in the timber industry, either in managing forests or processing timber.

Top Tip

Use spider diagrams to write down economic opportunities and economic limitations linked to land use in the mountains or along the coast.

Industry

Uplands are not particularly attractive to most industries because they lack flat building land and have poor communications by road, rail and sea. Industries such as mining and cement-making may be present. Coastal areas may have fishing industry or port developments which make a big impact on the local economy.

Military

Uplands and coastal areas are used for military training and for firing ranges due to their remote location.

Recreation and leisure

The recreation and leisure industry plays an increasingly large part in the land use profiles of upland and coastal areas. Activities such as rock and ice climbing, mountain biking, canoeing, sailing and skiing now take their place alongside the more traditional pursuits of fishing and shooting in the uplands and along the coast.

Tourism

Similarly, tourism is an important economic element in both the mountains and along the coast. Many jobs are provided in hotels, restaurants, shops and tourist attractions such as caves or beauty spots and tourist honeypots.

Water storage and supply

Deep valleys created by glaciers in hard rock are ideal for water storage to create hydroelectric power or to supply distant cities with water for homes and industries. High rainfall ensures a good, reliable supply. Ribbon lakes form natural reservoirs and water levels can be raised by building dams.

Top Tip

Use specific examples of conflicts based on the areas you studied in your class. Create a table that gives both sides of the conflict, their points of view and how the conflict might be solved.

Land use on OS maps

You should be able to identify these land uses on OS maps and work out possible conflicts that might arise in an area where people use the mountains or coastal landscapes for a variety of purposes.

Quick Test

1. Why are soils poor in mountain areas?

2. Why is forestry and growing trees a good use of mountain landscapes?

3. Why are mountain areas less suitable for industry?

4. In what ways do the mountains of Britain meet the needs of tourism and recreation?

Answers 1. They are often thin; the climate is cold and wet which impedes their development. **2.** Forests are suited to steeper mountain slopes and poorer soils. The natural landscape would be forested and they provide habitat for wildlife. **3.** There is not much flat land available for building. Communications by road and rail are often poor. There may be few raw materials nearby. **4.** There are many outdoor activities associated with mountains. They make good holiday destinations because of their scenery and amenities such as lakes and forests.

Land use conflicts in mountain and coastal environments

Conflicts over land use

Many people want to use the mountains, coast and open countryside to make their living or for leisure and recreation purposes. Others have an interest in preserving the landscape and natural environment. Often the way one group wishes to use the land conflicts with the wishes of another group.

See larger version on www.leckieandleckie.co.uk.

Conflicts and their causes

Reasons for conflict	Effects of conflict
Walkers damage walls and fences on farmer's land. Dogs attack livestock. Parking blocks lanes. Gates left open.	Farmers lose money due to livestock being killed by dogs or released onto busy roads. Walls and fences are expensive to repair.
Visitors disturb wildlife and cause damage to trees and plants, and this annoys conservationists and foresters. Deer management is affected.	Rare birds and animals are threatened. Forest fires cause loss of habitat and destroy valuable timber. Estates lose income.
Water sports enthusiasts create noise, pollution and bow waves on lakes and rivers.	Fishing is disrupted. Waterside trees and plants are undermined. People swimming are endangered by fast power boats. Polluted water must be treated before it is used for water supply at high expense.
Ski area developers take over large areas of land using roads and ugly ski equipment. Peace and quiet disrupted. Mountaineers and conservationists object.	Ugly landscape scars are visible from long distances spoiling views. Vegetation is trampled by visitors and skiers and is slow to recover. Wildlife is driven away.
Tourists visit honeypots creating traffic congestion and overcrowding. Local residents object because they find they are restricted by traffic jams and parked cars. Litter may be a problem.	Large vehicles such as caravans and motor homes block narrow roads or congest small towns and villages. Urgent journeys by locals such as doctors and nurses are slowed down by summer traffic. Parking is a problem for local residents.

Quick Test

Look at the above cartoon showing conflicts in the countryside.

a) For each of the problems shown create pairs of people likely to be in conflict. Choose from: farmer, tourist, water-skier, local resident, walker, mountain biker, water company official, motorist.

b) For two of the chosen pairs explain the reasons for the conflict

Answers Farmer – walker: walker damages fences and walls. Water-skier – tourist: noise from speed boats disturbs quiet of countryside. Local resident – motorist: motorist causes traffic congestion that may create problems for locals. Water company official – water-skier: speedboats may cause pollution. Mountain biker – farmer: bike can cause footpath erosion.

Resolving conflicts over land use

You need to be specific in looking at conflict resolution so check your class notes and the **conflicts you have studied**. Solutions to conflicts are often similar and usually involve people coming to agreement where everybody loses and gains a little.

- Motor boat conflict on Windermere resolved by imposing speed limits. Restrictions on boating bans power boats in favour of sail and paddles on other lakes. Water supply reservoirs like Thirlmere may ban boating and swimming. Boats and canoes slow when passing fishermen.
- Access agreements have been put in place in the Cairngorms and other ski resorts restricting where visitors and skiers can go in order to protect the natural environment.
- The Access to the Countryside Act lays out rights and responsibilities for people who own and use the land.
- Access is restricted by agreement during times when people are shooting and deerstalking.
- Footpath erosion is controlled by creating defined walking routes with footpaths. Gates and stiles are used to prevent damage to walls and fences. Mountain bikes and off-road vehicles are banned from certain routes and locations in National Parks.
- Wildlife and nature reserves are created with special protection. Sites of Special Scientific Interest are created by the Government.

Agencies and voluntary bodies

There are a number of government agencies and voluntary bodies involved in countryside issues.

Government agencies include Scottish Natural Heritage, English Heritage and National Park authorities. These bodies regulate land use in the countryside and work with people to protect the natural environment. The Forestry Commission looks after woodlands and forests.

Voluntary bodies are charities who involve themselves in protecting wildlife and natural heritage. Examples are the National Trust and the National Trust for Scotland (owners of historic buildings and nature reserves), the Royal Society for the Protection of Birds (RSPB) and the Wildlife Trust (protection of birds and wildlife).

Quick Test

1. Why do conflicts happen over land use in the countryside?
2. Give examples of ways in which visitors can affect wildlife in a mountain area.
3. How can too many visitors affect a coastal area you have studied?

Answers 1. Because people have different views and needs when using the countryside. **2.** Skiers may drive wildlife away; climbers may affect nesting birds on cliffs; food waste may encourage predators which take other birds' eggs; pollution may affect river ecology. **3.** In areas like the Dorset coast too many visitors cause congestion at honeypots like Lulworth Cove and Durdle Door. Caravans in Pembrokeshire spoil the scenery when they occupy large caravan parks. Small towns like Swanage in Dorset suffer from traffic management problems in the summer holidays.

OS maps in the exam

The exam paper involves using and interpreting 1:25 000 or 1:50 000 Ordnance Survey maps and you will need to be able to use the range of mapping skills detailed in the checklist below.

Mapping and practical skills checklist

Required skill	Tick
Using 4 and 6 figure grid references *	
Measure straight line distances	
Annotate, label and interpret cross sections *	
Use contours to interpret height and steepness of slope *	
Describe, interpret and analyse relief and landscape patterns * **EXAMPLES:** glaciated, limestone, river and coastal landscapes	
Interpret transport patterns	
Analyse and interpret land use zones within settlements **EXAMPLES:** CBD, old industrial areas, new industrial areas, housing patterns	
Describe and give reasons for land use *	
Identify and explain potential land use conflicts *	
Use maps in association with photographs/field sketches, cross sections/transects	
Interpret and annotate field sketches and photographs	
* in the exam	

Top Tip

Improve your map-reading skills through participation in scouts and guides, the Duke of Edinburgh Award or cadets.

Top Tip

The map extract used in the exam is complete with a key so you don't have to remember what each map symbol represents. However, it is a good idea to be familiar with the map key before the exam.

Top Tip

Practical experience of map reading out in the field or on an expedition cannot be beaten. Spend some time outdoors using the OS map.

Using contours

The diagram, **Landscape features and contour patterns on OS maps** shows some of the main landscape elements and the contour patterns that go with them. You should know these and be able to spot them on maps.

See larger version on www.leckieandleckie.co.uk.

Landscape features and contour patterns on OS maps

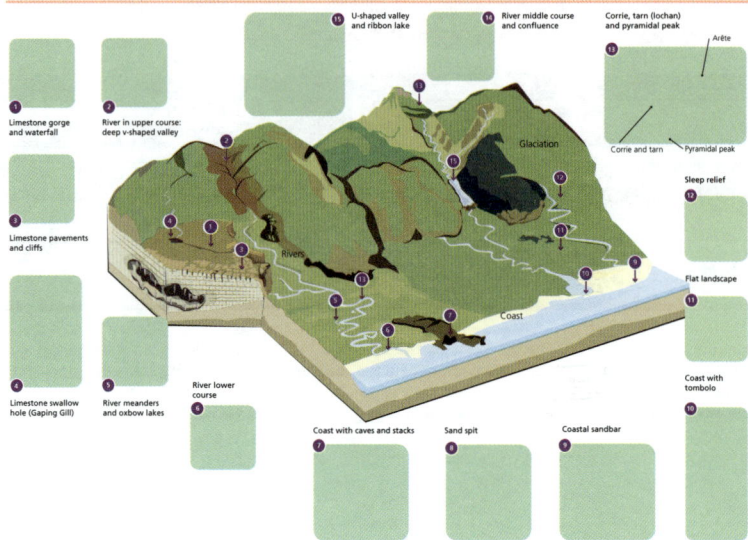

Using transects and cross-sections

Cross-sections or transects are used in most exam papers at this level to get you to identify features on the Ordnance Survey map. These may be landscape features or land uses in a rural or urban environment.

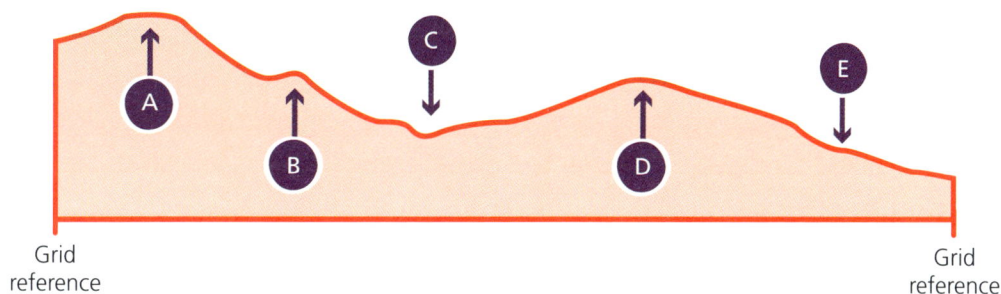

Grid reference

Grid reference

Recognising different land uses

It is important to be able to recognise different land uses on Ordnance Survey maps and to know where to look for them.

- **Hill farming**

  Found among areas of mountain and moorland with steep slopes. These low population areas have poor, badly drained soils.

- **Arable farming**

  Lowland well drained areas; farms dotted about among the fields.

- **Commercial forestry**

  Large blocks of forest with forest tracks to provide access. Often on steeper slopes with high rainfall and poorer soils.

- **Extractive industry**

  Mining and quarrying may be in upland, lowland or urban areas. Look for large buildings, railway lines, canals and waste heaps.

- **Industrial sites**

  Often found in urban areas. Old industry tends to be found in the run-down inner city, next to docks, railways and canals or on coalfields. New industry is more likely to be on the edge of towns next to major roads.

- **CBD (Central Business District)**

  Found where roads converge in the city centre. Look for many churches and dark outlined public buildings such as the town hall. Look for tourist information centres, main transport termini and universities. Street patterns may be grid iron.

- **Residential areas**

  Old tenement and terraced housing is found in the inner city next to the older industrial sites detailed above; look for grid iron patterns of streets. Newer housing is found on the edge of town unless there has been inner city renewal. It is recognised by its rounded terrace patterns and green space.

- **Recreational areas**

  Often located in mountain areas and National Parks, identified with blue map symbols indicating such things as viewpoints, campsites and nature trails. Large developments such as ski resorts have ski lifts and buildings.

- **Other land uses**

  It is possible to spot other land uses such as hydroelectric schemes, reservoirs, petrochemical plants and sewage works.

Glaciated mountains and landscape features

The Cairngorm OS map shows a typical glaciated area in the British Isles. You will need to be able to identify glacial features using grid references, say what they look like and explain how they were formed. Can you spot these features on the map? *Corrie, tarn/corrie loch, pyramidal peak, arête, U-shaped valley, misfit stream, truncated spur, hanging valley, ribbon lake/loch.*

Grid reference	Glaciated landscape feature		Grid reference	Glaciated landscape feature
964026	U-shaped valley		988035	Arête
993037	Misfit stream		004026	Hanging valley
981028	Corrie and lochan		012022	Ribbon loch

Glaciated mountains, land use and land use conflicts

The map extract shows many typical land uses found in the mountains and these may well be involved in land use conflict situations. Note the Cairngorm ski area – the map and photos (see p36) show examples of how this activity makes a large impact on the landscape. Conservationists value this area for its high landscape value and its wildlife interest. Its position in the Cairngorms National Park poses interesting questions.

Loch Morlich and the Queen's Forest are of similar interest. Note the variety of land use around the loch. Large numbers of visitors undoubtedly have an effect on the forest, its management and wildlife. Mountaineers, climbers and hillwalkers use this area and can create problems like footpath erosion. The many car parks, cycle trails, viewpoints and the funicular railway all suggest potentially crowded pressure points known as honeypots.

Wildlife in this area is very important with rare birds like the dotterel, golden eagle and snow bunting living here. The forest is a native Caledonian pine forest and is the habitat for a wide range of creatures such as deer, pine martens, red squirrel and black grouse. Large numbers of deer roam the hills and some estates use these and grouse as the basis of hunting and shooting. Lochs and rivers are ideal habitats for water birds, trout and salmon.

Mountain Land use

1. Corrie
2. Hydroelectric scheme
3. Loch

Ski lifts give easy access to the summits.

Military training causes noise and disturbance.

High mountain life such as ptarmigan and dotterel.

Crags used for rock climbing and ice climbing

Breeding grounds for peregrine falcon and golden eagle

Nature reserves are set up to protect wildlife.

Corries hold snow, ideal for skiing.

Footpath erosion creates landscape scars.

Visual impact of lifts

Valley flooded by HEP scheme.

Commercial forests in straight lines. Little wildlife here.

Large numbers of red deer – important income for shooting estates.

Ski areas and hydroelectric schemes spoil the landscape.

Visitors cross farmland and damage crops and fences.

Hang-gliding

Power lines and super pylons spoil the view.

Deer may graze on farmland and destroy crops.

Water may become polluted.

Visitors may pose fire-risks to forest plantations.

Traffic may be a problem around honeypots.

Power boats may conflict with other water users.

Small towns attract visitors but may have traffic congestion problems.

Town depends on tourist income.

Camp and caravan sites are a visual intrusion.

Water birds rely on lochs and water margins.

Historic houses are visitor attractions.

Natural forest and woodland is good wildlife habitat.

See larger version on www.leckieandleckie.co.uk.

Cairngorm ski area

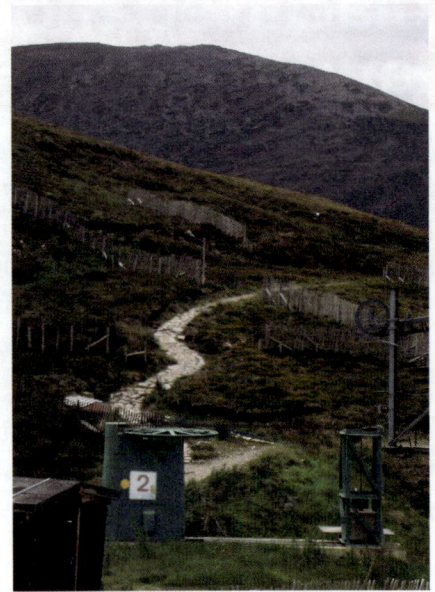
Ski area footpath

Quick Test

1. Use the map and the mountain land use diagram to identify land uses typical of mountain areas.

2. Enter grid references in the table below that locate the land uses found on the map.

Cairngorm land use	Grid ref.
Ski area	
Funicular railway	
Water sports centre	
Climbing – corrie rock faces	
Mountain biking trail	

3. List conflicts that might occur on the map area over land use.

Physical Environments exam-style questions

1. Using map evidence, describe and explain the advantages and environmental impact of tourism on the area shown in the Cairngorm map extract. **(6)**

2. Study the Ordnance Survey map extract of the Cairngorms on page 34.

   a) Describe the physical features of the river Allt Creag an Leth-choin from 972032 to where it enters Loch Morlich at 970093. **(4)**

   b) Identify the feature of glacial erosion found at each of the grid references below.

   964026   981028   988035   004026

   Choose from:

   corrie and lochan   arête   hanging valley   U-shaped valley **(3)**

   c) Explain how a corrie is formed.

   You may use a diagram(s) to illustrate your answer. **(4)**

   Cross-section XY from GR 973098 to 998039

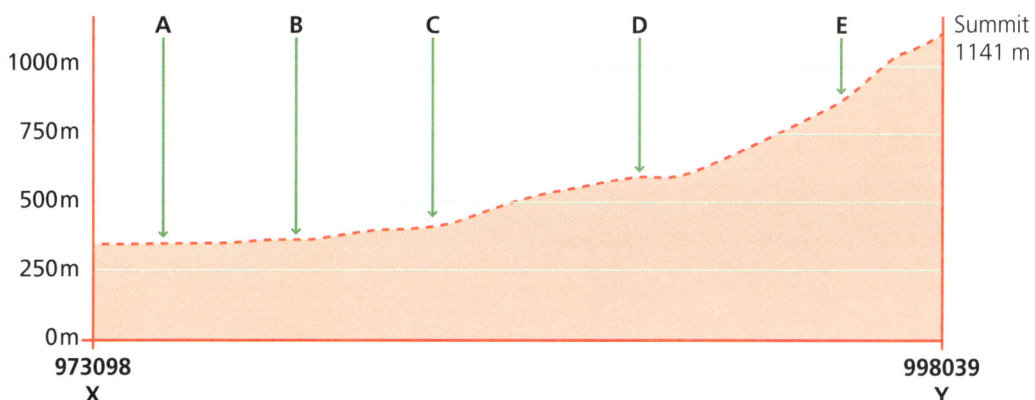

   d) Study the Ordnance Survey map of the Cairngorms and the reference diagram.

   i) Match the letters shown on the transect X-Y above to the land features and land uses listed below.

   ski area   river   forest edge   Fiacaill a' Coire Cais   forest track **(3)**

   ii) To what extent do you agree that ski development may be at conflict with other land uses in the area of the map extract?

   Give reasons to support your answer. **(4)**

   e) Using map evidence:

   i) describe the leisure and tourism features available on the map; **(3)**

   ii) explain the benefits these leisure and tourism features bring to the area. **(4)**

   Total 25 marks

Task

1. Create a short marking scheme to the question above using bullet points for answers.
2. Mark the completed answer and see how many marks it should score.

Human Environment: Unit outcomes

In this unit you will study how people relate to and develop their environment. You will need to develop your skills in handling geographical information. You will be expected to understand how people interact with their environment. The unit is about thinking critically and using graphical information. It will test your ability to handle maps, diagrams and written summaries. You will also be expected to handle basic statistical information.

Skills checklist

You should be familiar with the following skills:

- Interpretation and annotation of field sketches and photos
- Four figure and six figure grid references
- Measurement of distances on maps
- Using and interpreting contours, contour patterns and measuring height on maps
- Analysing transport routes
- Analysing and interpreting land use zones within settlements
- Interpretation of land use patterns
- Identification and explanation of conflicts
- Using maps in association with photos, field sketches, cross-sections and transects

Map skills are based on 1:50 000 and 1:25 000 scale Ordnance Survey maps.

Top Tip
Use the skills list here as a checklist. Tick off all the ones you are comfortable with. Target any others for extra practice and revision.

Techniques checklist

- Being familiar with and able to complete maps involving choropleths, isolines and proportional symbols.
- Using and interpreting graphs – line, bar, scatter, pie.
- Being able to use data from surveys and questionnaires.

Top Tip
Pay special attention to the key that goes with any map or diagram. It provides vital help and prompting for you. Similarly, read all the labels and annotations on graphics in the exam **carefully** as they provide clues.

World population distribution

Factors influencing population distribution and density

The world's population is not evenly spread. Population density is a measure of the number of people living in a square kilometre. Areas with lots of people are called high population density areas; areas with few people are called low population density areas. We might also refer to them as densely populated areas and sparsely populated areas. The map below shows that some places have low population density with less than 20 people per km^2 and other parts of the world seem crowded with over 260 people per km^2.

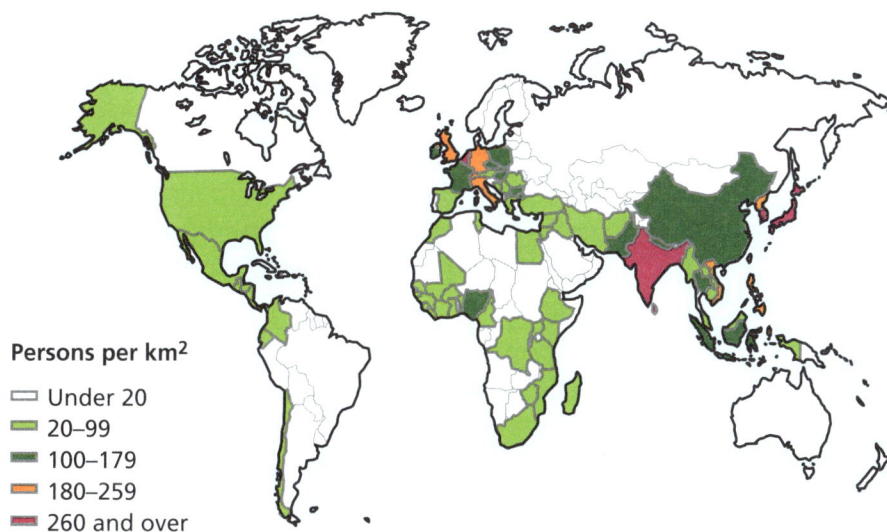

Persons per km^2
- Under 20
- 20–99
- 100–179
- 180–259
- 260 and over

To explain why some places have more people living in each km^2 and others have less you should take into account the following factors.

- **Relief** – This involves the shape of the land and whether it has steep or gentle slopes.

- **Climate** – There are a number of different climate zones around the world. Some encourage people to live in a place while others create a challenging environment.

- **Resources** – Good farmland, sources of energy like oil or coal and useful minerals such as metals all encourage people to settle in an area.

- **Employment opportunities** – Areas offering people the chance to find well paid work are more likely to attract people than those areas where people find little opportunity to earn money to support their families.

These elements determining population density are both **physical and human factors** but they are often linked. For example, having plenty of resources (physical factor) is likely to lead to employment opportunities (human factor) in an area, so population density will increase. By way of a contrast, areas with steep relief and harsh climate (physical factors) will be poor land for farming providing few jobs (human factor), so population density is likely to remain low.

Top Tip
Make good use of maps by identifying countries and regions on them to use as examples in your exam answers. Learn where places are on the maps and use them as you are revising.

Explaining differences in population density

The map above shows a range of population densities by identifying particular areas. You should be able to explain why these areas have a low or a high population density. The table below matches the numbers on the map to named areas and provides a brief explanation of the low or high density figures shown.

Area	Explanation of high or low population density figures
Western Europe	High population density: fertile soils and relatively low relief provide good farming conditions. Good resource base of energy supplies and minerals. Well developed road, rail and shipping networks. EMDCs with employment in industries and services.
Indian subcontinent	High population density due to the ability of the land to support a large population. India has over 1 billion people. Fertile lowlands like the valleys of the Indus and Ganges rivers provide farmlands. The monsoon climate provides rainfall which can be stored and used in irrigation schemes. The tropical climate allows up to three crops per year under irrigation.
Amazonia	Low population density due to the challenging equatorial climate of high temperatures and heavy rainfall. This makes the soils relatively poor for commercial farming. Dense forest and steep relief make settlement and communications difficult. Resources are undeveloped or are exported from the area, providing few jobs.
Australia	Low population density due to hostile living conditions away from the coast. Large areas of desert and semi-desert have largely limited settlement to mining towns or those with specific water supplies.
Sahara desert	Low population density due to desert climate and challenging landscape conditions. Populations cluster around oases and mineral resources or oil fields. Poor road networks and limited water supplies restrict farming and industrial development.
Japan and Korea	High population density: here highly developed industrial economies import raw materials and produce a wide range of goods for home supply and for export. Employment opportunities support large, relatively wealthy populations in urban areas. Highly developed transport and communications systems encourage economic development. Restrictions imposed by steep relief are met by hi-tech solutions such as tunnelling, bridge building and major land reclamation schemes.

Contrasting rural and urban populations

World population density maps need to be used with caution because there can be big differences in population density within countries. Refer to the population density map and you will notice that the United States of America has a low density of population overall. In reality, there are areas with very high population densities like the giant cities of the east coast, for example New York or Washington, or the huge urban sprawl of San Francisco and Los Angeles on the west coast. Alaska, on the other hand, is one of the least populated areas on earth, but the map would lead you to conclude otherwise. It should be noted that in the year 2000 79% of US citizens lived in urban areas. None of these high population areas show up on the map.

Similarly, the map of Japan does not show the mainly mountainous interior with its low population density. The picture is distorted by the large urban population concentrated around the coastal lowlands.

Quick Test

1. What are the physical and human factors that account for differences in population density and distribution shown on the world map?

2. Why does most of the world's population live on coastal or river plains?

Answers 1. Answers could include: relief; climate; communications such as roads, ports and air links; employment; raw materials and water supplies. **2.** These areas provide lowlands suitable for farming and may provide the best soils. They also allow good communications by road, rail and sea.

World population change

Population growth

Population growth varies between EMDCs, which have low growth, and ELDCs, which have high growth rates. Population statistics show growth rates over time, changing population structures and variations in growth rates. It is important to be able to understand the factors that affect change and interpret the likely effects of change.

Using statistics

Population statistics for selected countries 2008

Country	CBR per 1000	CMR per 1000	IMR per 1000 live births	Life expectancy at birth
Bangladesh	29	8	57	63
Botswana	23	14	44	50
Brazil	19	6	23	72
Canada	10	8	5	81
Ethiopia	44	12	83	55
France	13	8	3	81
Germany	8	4	3	79
Malaysia	22	5	16	73
Niger	50	20	115	50
Pakistan	28	8	67	64
Poland	10	10	7	75
Saudi Arabia	29	2	12	76

Source US Census Bureau http://www.census.gov/ipc/www/idb/

The statistics reveal a lot about the differences between EMDCs and ELDCs. **Crude Birth Rate** (CBR) is the numbers of babies being born in a year, while **Crude Mortality Rate** (CMR) is the number of deaths recorded in that year, each given in terms of per 1000 head of population.

Interpreting the statistics

Some of the factors behind these statistics are as follows:

• ELDCs have high birth rates due to cultural pressures to have many children. Children are needed to help work the land or provide family income. Many children die young so it is important to have a large family to be sure some survive. Children look after parents when they become elderly as other care is often unavailable. There may be a lack of available contraception or religious objections to using artificial birth control.

• ELDCs have high death rates because poor health services mean that people are more likely to die of disease and injuries. Water quality is likely to be poor, leading to gastrointestinal (diarrhoeal) diseases, which is a major factor affecting the **infant mortality rate** (IMR). Death rates may be high because of infectious diseases such as malaria, cholera, polio, typhoid and HIV infection.

- EMDCs have low birth rates because cultural pressures encourage smaller families. Better health services ensure survival of infants as shown by low IMR. Vaccination eliminates most childhood diseases. Contraception is widely available and both men and women work to achieve a good lifestyle. This tends to restrict the number of children born to each couple.

- EMDCs have low death rates. Public health policies target diseases such as sexually transmitted infections, coronary heart disease and cancer to extend life expectancy. Infectious diseases are prevented, treated and under control.

Infant mortality rate and **life expectancy at birth** figures reflect these factors. The economically secure lifestyle, good health and nutrition of EMDCs prolong life and reduce IMR. Poverty, malnutrition, poor water quality and poor living conditions lead to high IMR and lower life expectancy in ELDCs.

The demographic transition model shows how population growth, and in some cases decline, varies between ELDCs with high birth and death rates and the EMDCs with low birth and death rates. At either end of the model (sections A and D) birth rates and death rates fluctuate so that if there are more deaths than births the population of a country will fall. In both cases though, there is overall population stability with little increase or decline. In sections B and C there is a big difference between birth and death rate so population growth occurs.

This transition has happened with EMDCs but there is a question mark over whether it will be the experience of the poor nations in the early stage of the model.

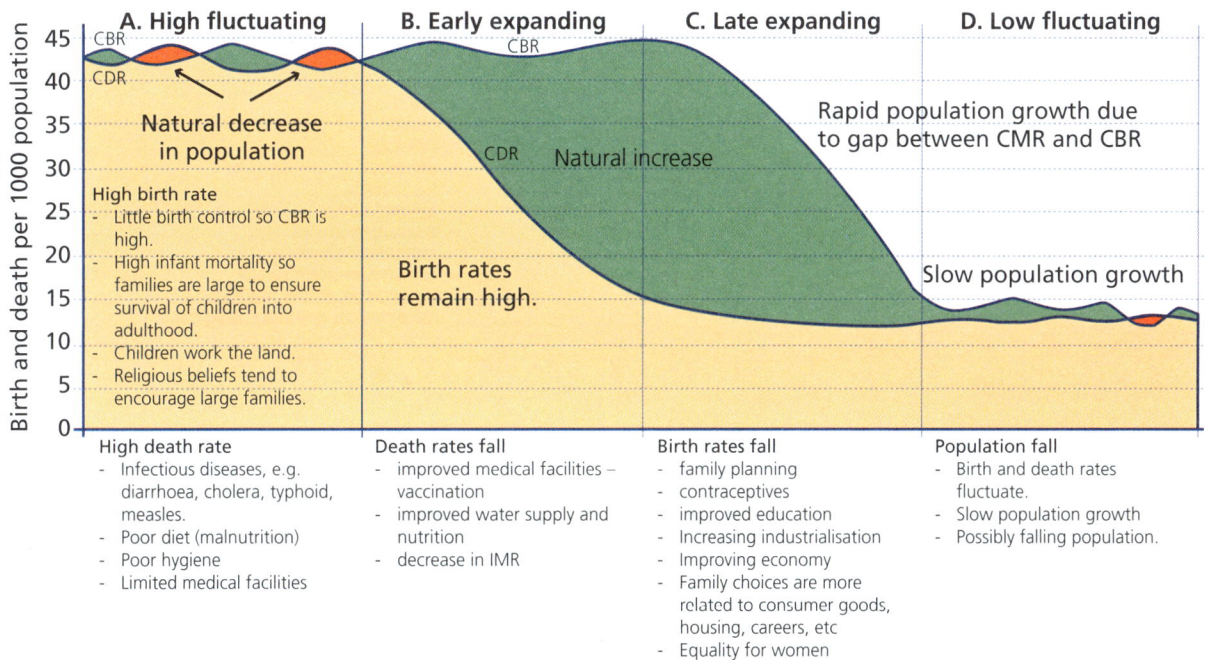

A. High fluctuating	B. Early expanding	C. Late expanding	D. Low fluctuating

Birth and death per 1000 population (y-axis: 0–45)

CBR
CDR

Natural decrease in population

High birth rate
- Little birth control so CBR is high.
- High infant mortality so families are large to ensure survival of children into adulthood.
- Children work the land.
- Religious beliefs tend to encourage large families.

CDR   Natural increase

Birth rates remain high.

CBR

Rapid population growth due to gap between CMR and CBR

Slow population growth

High death rate
- Infectious diseases, e.g. diarrhoea, cholera, typhoid, measles.
- Poor diet (malnutrition)
- Poor hygiene
- Limited medical facilities

Death rates fall
- improved medical facilities – vaccination
- improved water supply and nutrition
- decrease in IMR

Birth rates fall
- family planning
- contraceptives
- improved education
- Increasing industrialisation
- Improving economy
- Family choices are more related to consumer goods, housing, careers, etc
- Equality for women

Population fall
- Birth and death rates fluctuate.
- Slow population growth
- Possibly falling population.

Quick Test

1. Why do ELDCs have high birth rates?

2. Why is the infant mortality rate a good indicator of development?

3. What is the main cause of infant deaths in ELDCs?

4. What does the demographic transition model show?

Answers 1. Lack of available birth control: children are needed to work to support the family. **2.** Because children are among the most vulnerable citizens and are more likely to die from disease and hardship. **3.** Diarrhoeal diseases caused by poor water supplies. **4.** It shows the relationship between CBR and CMR over time and reveals population growth and decline.

Population structure

Population pyramids and changing structure over time

Population pyramids provide a breakdown of the age groupings of a population in a given year. These diagrams are used to interpret past, present and future events in the growth of a population. The pyramid is divided into male and female populations and each generation of people born over time is shown. The top of the pyramid shows the older generations (**elderly dependants**) while the base of the pyramid shows the very young children in the society (**young dependants**). The middle of the pyramid shows the **working population**, usually those over 16 years and below retirement age (normally 65 years).

Top Tip
Read graphs carefully. Be sure to include figures taken from them in exam answers.

Chad: 2008	Population in millions. Source: US Census Bureau, International database.

■ Male
■ Female

Narrow top of the pyramid shows life expectancy

Small working population compared to the young dependants

Many young dependants shows high birth rate and growing population

Broad base to pyramid: need for more education and child health services

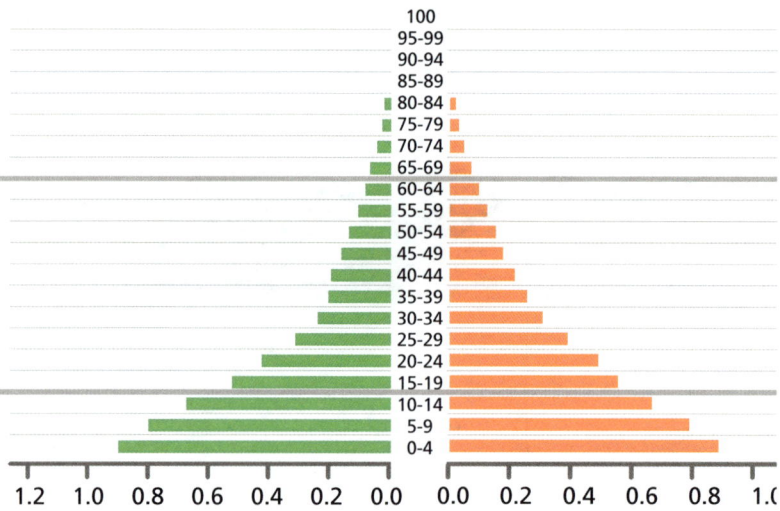

100
95-99
90-94
85-89
80-84
75-79
70-74
65-69
60-64
55-59
50-54
45-49
40-44
35-39
30-34
25-29
20-24
15-19
10-14
5-9
0-4

1.2 1.0 0.8 0.6 0.4 0.2 0.0   0.0 0.2 0.4 0.6 0.8 1.0

Germany: 2008	Population in millions. Source: US Census Bureau, International database.

■ Male
■ Female

Possible need for more elderly care

Broad top of the pyramid shows high life expectancy

Large generation will become elderly dependents in the future

Large but declining working population

Narrow base reflects level of birth control

Narrow base suggests a smaller working population in the future

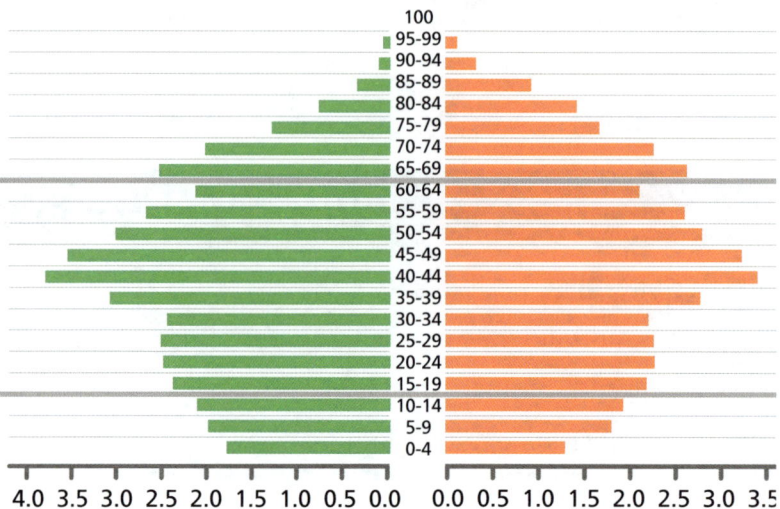

100
95-99
90-94
85-89
80-84
75-79
70-74
65-69
60-64
55-59
50-54
45-49
40-44
35-39
30-34
25-29
20-24
15-19
10-14
5-9
0-4

4.0 3.5 3.0 2.5 2.0 1.5 1.0 0.5 0.0   0.0 0.5 1.0 1.5 2.0 2.5 3.0 3.5

Population trends

The pyramids can be used to predict what is likely to happen in a country in the near future. Large numbers of young dependants means there will be a need for more health care services for children and mothers. It also means that there will be a need to create more school places. A growing population will require a greater amount of food and other resources. Large generations in the middle years and large numbers of elderly dependants suggest a need for more elderly care so resources will need to be switched from providing school and health care for the young. A declining working population is a concern as these are the people who provide for the young and elderly dependants through the taxes they pay.

Top Tip
Look for high points and low points in graphs and make note of where lines become steeper or flatter (trends). Try to be systematic when describing and explaining what graphs show by writing things in a logical order.

Working age population

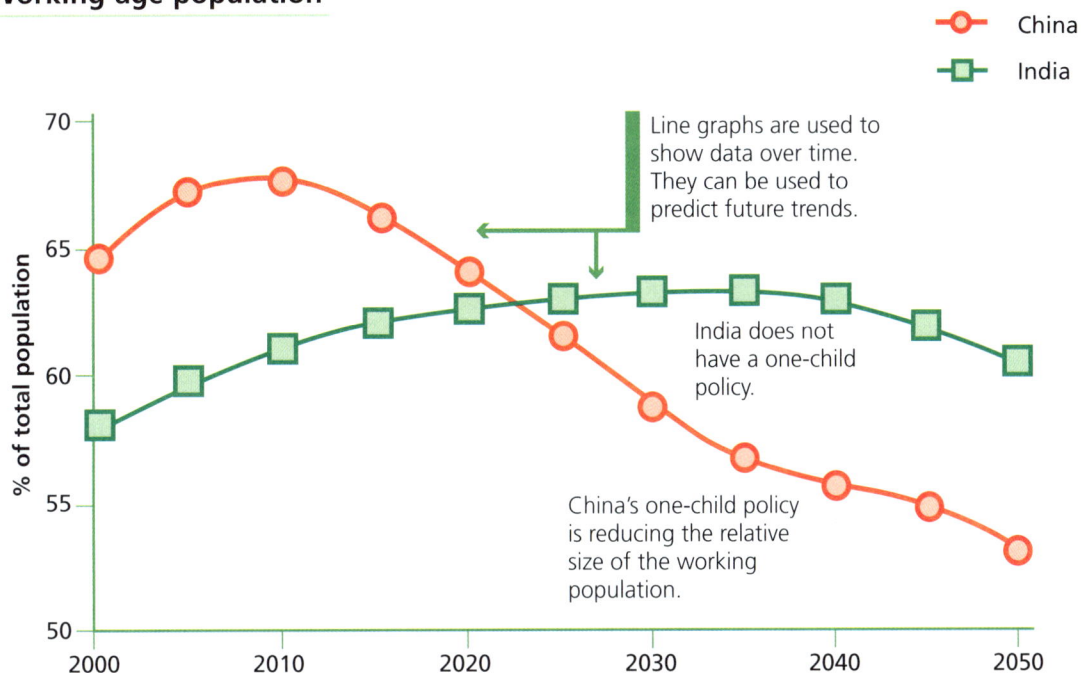

Line graphs are used to show data over time. They can be used to predict future trends.

India does not have a one-child policy.

China's one-child policy is reducing the relative size of the working population.

Future trends: India and China

India and China are the two most populated countries on the planet, each with over 1 billion people. The effects of China's one child policy can be seen in the rapid decline of its percentage working population. Strict enforcement of the policy has clearly had the effect of bringing population under control. India does not have the same policy, although birth control on a voluntary basis has been government policy since the 1970s. India shows a similar trend but with a less steep decline in working population in the future. It is important to remember that these are percentage figures and the **actual numbers** of working people will continue to increase into the foreseeable future.

Other ways of representing population trends

Using a variety of graphs can help in interpreting population trends.

Numbers of people in specific age groups in the UK

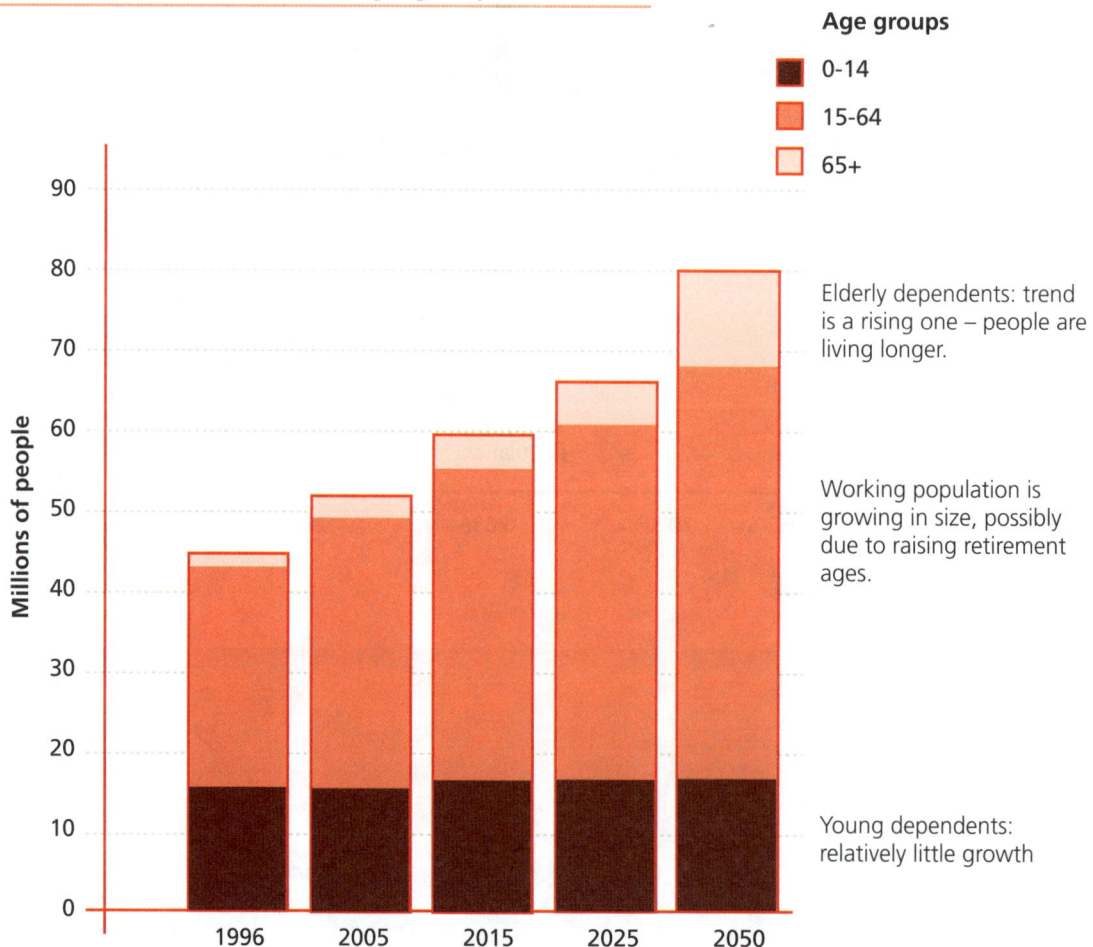

Age groups
- ■ 0-14
- ■ 15-64
- ■ 65+

Elderly dependents: trend is a rising one – people are living longer.

Working population is growing in size, possibly due to raising retirement ages.

Young dependents: relatively little growth

The divided bar graph showing the total numbers in various age groups in the UK both past and present helps governments and businesses to plan ahead. Each group makes its own particular demands on the economy. Noting the growing number of elderly people or people in the working population should allow the government to get its future planning right. Pictographs provide a good visual representation of a set of statistics so that things can be seen at a glance.

Pictograph: male and female literacy in the Philippines

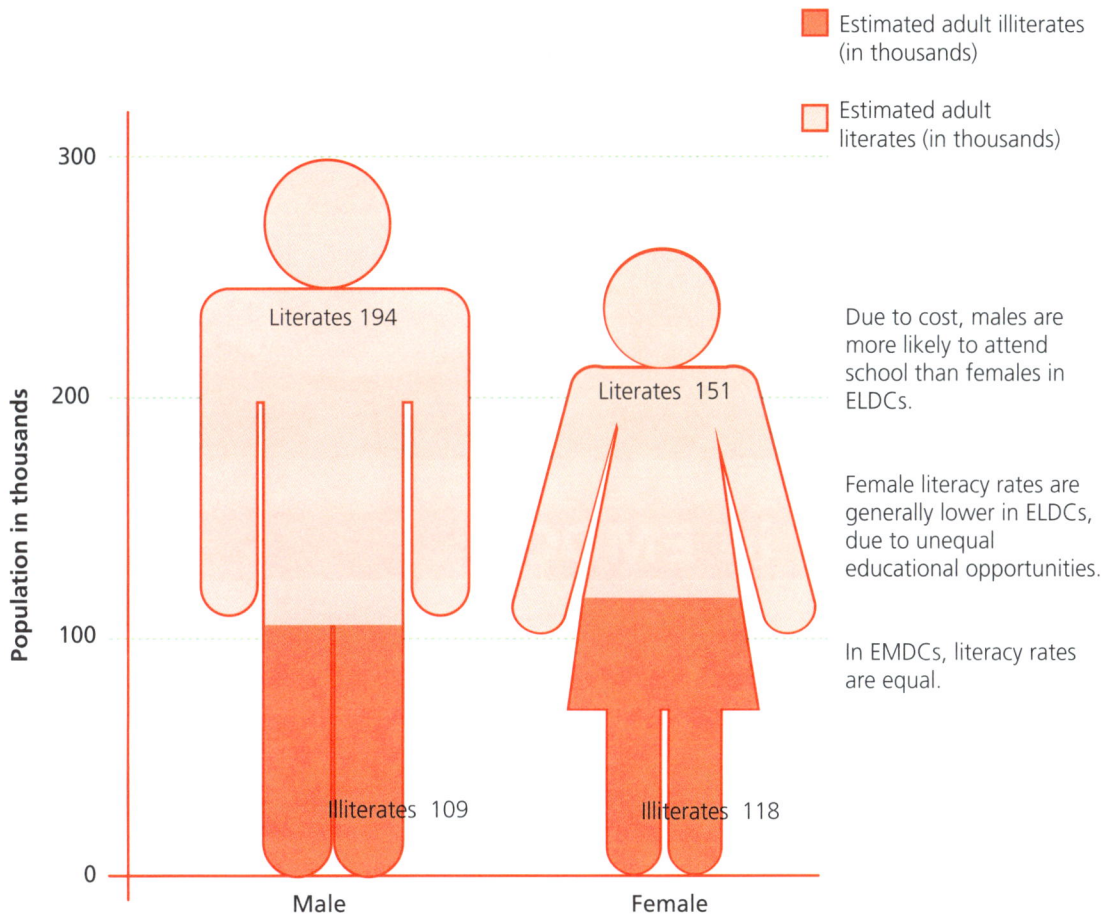

Estimated adult illiterates (in thousands)

Estimated adult literates (in thousands)

Population in thousands

Literates 194

Literates 151

Illiterates 109

Illiterates 118

Male

Female

Due to cost, males are more likely to attend school than females in ELDCs.

Female literacy rates are generally lower in ELDCs, due to unequal educational opportunities.

In EMDCs, literacy rates are equal.

Quick Test

1. What does the wide base of the population pyramid for Chad in Africa show?

2. Why is the base on the German pyramid narrower than the middle?

3. What steps will the German government need to take to deal with the possible problems in the future due to the population structure shown?

4. Why is the adult literacy rate in Chad likely to stay low in the future?

Answers 1. The wide base shows a high crude birth rate (CBR). **2.** This shows the effect of birth control in the past which has translated into smaller generations compared to other areas of the population pyramid. **3.** Population pyramids allow governments to set new priorities for spending, so answers could include more health care for the elderly or changes in tax rates. **4.** The high birth rate will mean that resources will not be available to pay for the education of so many children. There is also likely to be a difference in the numbers of boys rather than girls being educated.

Urban change in EMDCs

Urban areas in EMDCs involve a number of issues all relating to development and response to change. Urban development depends on economics and planning control which limits the ways the land in the city is used. Models of cities are often used to show land use zones and to explain why they develop.

Key

- CBD
- Factory zone/zone in transition
- Zone of working men's homes
- Residential zone

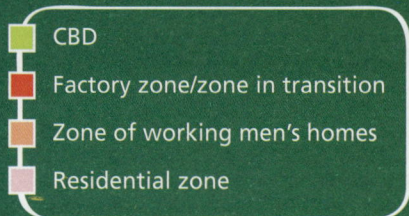

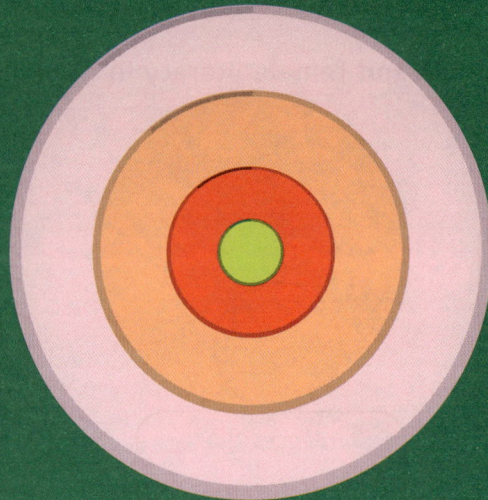

All of these models contain areas known as functional zones. These are areas where one particular function (e.g. retailing/commercial, industry, different types of housing) dominate.

Urban issues in EMDCs

- Housing – **inner city** housing has seen a great deal of change. These areas originally housed industrial workers and were found next to factories, docks, railways and canals. As old, heavy, city-based industry declined, large areas of old **slum housing** were cleared or redeveloped (**gentrification**). Replacement housing was built on the cleared space and the **central business district (CBD)** expanded into the inner city, e.g. London Docklands and Glasgow's Eastern Area Renewal Scheme (GEAR). New housing estates have grown up around the edges of cities where land prices are lower and greenfield sites are available for new developments. Large **local authority housing** areas were built here on cities' edges to provide replacement homes for those cleared from the inner city. Inner city areas still provide cheaper housing and may be used by students and newer arrivals to the city (in-migration). This can have the effect of creating areas made up of specific ethnic groups (**ghettoisation**).

- Transport – new road systems have been developed to cope with the high volumes of motor vehicles trying to enter cities. These allow better access to city centres and help to avoid traffic congestion. **Ring roads** direct through traffic around the outside of towns and avoid the congested centre. **Inner ring roads** keep other vehicles out of the CBD. Urban motorways and fast highways are used to speed traffic flow. Some cities have introduced **congestion charges** so that only those with a pressing need will choose to enter the city centre. Public transport systems using buses, trams and commuter railways attempt to reduce reliance on cars.

Top Tip
You should try to relate these issues to the urban area you have studied in your course.

- Retail and commercial development – recent years have seen a trend towards developing large out-of-town retail and commercial outlets. These require a lot of space so the cheaper **greenfield sites** next to the main routes on the edge of town are ideal as consumers depend on cars to access them. Retail parks and malls compete with the existing town centre shops which have **higher overheads** (city taxes, high cost land). This has led to a decline in some city centres as shops and supermarkets move out. Modern **industrial estates** rely on transport too so the edge of town is now their most likely location. Some industrial and commercial development may take place in the inner city, taking over old industrial land (**brownfield sites**). Pre-used and derelict sites provide cheap land and may attract government or city grants to encourage development and to provide new jobs, e.g. Braehead in Glasgow, the Gyle Centre and Edinburgh Park in Edinburgh, Brent Cross in London.

- Environmental quality – serious problems relating to pollution are experienced by most large cities. Poor air quality is associated with traffic congestion and this leads to **smog** which has a bad effect on people's health. To overcome this, a number of solutions have proved effective. Park and ride systems and congestion charging have reduced traffic volumes in inner city areas.

- **Pedestrianisation** has created a better city centre shopping environment by separating people and traffic. Inner-city multi-storey or underground car parks reduce on-street parking, which reduces traffic flow. Parking restrictions, parking meters and bus and cycle lanes all discriminate against the motorist and favour other means of accessing the city centre. Cities have large carbon footprints and make a major contribution to global warming. Governments have commitments to deal with this problem so land use in the city is likely to continue to change.

Top Tip
You should be able to spot the features discussed on this page on OS maps.

Quick Test

1. In the city or urban area you have studied, what changes have recently taken place in the inner city?

2. Why does pedestrianisation create a better urban environment for people?

3. Why might a greenfield site be more attractive to a developer than a brownfield site?

Answers 1. Answers could include: urban renewal, house building and gentrification and development of small industrial units to replace old heavy industries. 2. Separating people and traffic creates a safer urban environment and cuts down atmospheric pollution. Traffic congestion is reduced too. 3. Greenfield sites are cheaper to develop as there are issues such as old derelict buildings or environmental waste to deal with.

Urban change in ELDCs

Urban areas in ELDCs experience similar issues to those cities in the more developed countries and likewise involve development and response to change. Urban development in ELDCs still depends on economics and planning but also has to take into account the pressure of rapid population growth associated with cities in the developing world. The urban models for cities in developing countries show a number of differences from those for cities in the developed world. In particular, there are large areas of poor quality housing and informal **shantytown** developments that cause serious problems for governments and city authorities. Cities in ELDCs often show a large gap in living conditions between the rich urban elite and the masses of poor people who live close together.

LEDC urban land use model

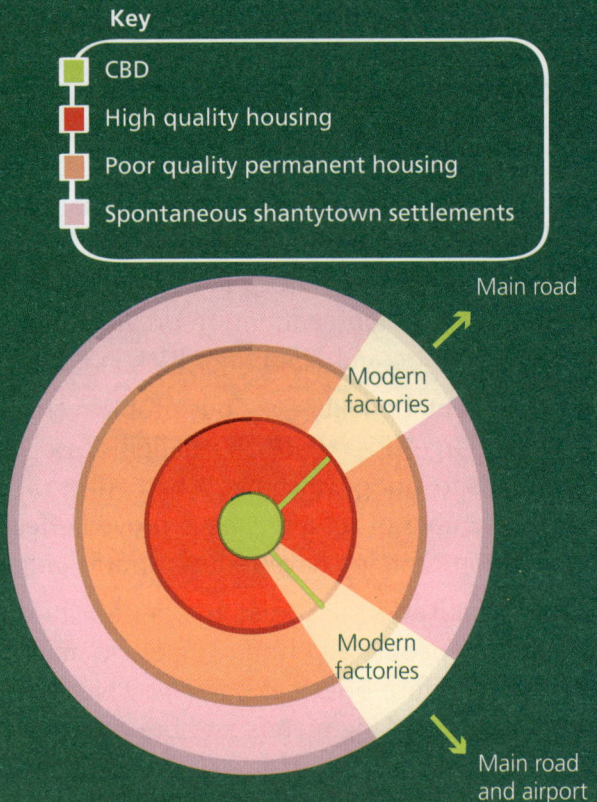

Key
- CBD
- High quality housing
- Poor quality permanent housing
- Spontaneous shantytown settlements

Main road

Modern factories

Modern factories

Main road and airport

Urban issues in ELDCs

- Housing – the poverty of the slum housing areas contrasts with the urban environment found in protected housing districts set behind protective security fences. Shantytowns are unplanned housing areas set up by squatters. They develop as new arrivals to the city find it difficult to rent or buy proper housing. For example in Brazil, São Paulo has extensive shanty areas (**favelas**). They lack amenities such as schools and health centres, and have poor water, sewerage and electricity services. Problems of violence, gang-related crime, drug abuse, prostitution and poor public health exist.

- Transport – motor vehicles create congestion and pollution problems. Public transport is densely packed with commuters and often is under severe strain. Unless regulated, traffic will tend to quickly **gridlock** poorly planned and developed road systems. Railways, tram systems and buses provide vital links into the centre and are accessible to the poor. Many people use bicycles, motorbikes and scooters to move around cities.

- Environmental quality – air pollution and water pollution from factories, traffic and housing create a dangerous urban environment with serious health risks. In São Paulo too rapid growth has made organising and planning developments difficult. In contrast, the city centre (CBD) may compare well with European or North American cities with many of the same shops and features. Waste disposal creates large rubbish dumps on the edge of town. These may provide opportunities for poor people (often children) to recycle the rubbish to earn a living. Water sanitation and infrastructure is a problem because without proper infrastructure sewage and waste are not easily disposed of. Poorer housing areas experience high rates of infant mortality, disease and ill health. Water-borne diseases such as typhoid and yellow fever may become epidemic. Wealthy areas of São Paulo will have good services but, as in many ELDCs, electricity supply may be intermittent or may only be available for a few hours each day in the favelas. Squatters often steal electricity by illegally hooking up to the electric supply.

Improving the urban environment: São Paulo, Brazil

- Counter urbanisation – people move out of town to satellite new towns and commute to the city.
- Shantytown dwellers work together on self-help schemes which use basic materials to provide sound replacement buildings for the shanties.
- City authorities and power companies provide cheap networked electricity to the improved areas.
- Safe water is piped into housing districts; sewerage and waste systems are set up.
- Health clinics and education services improve social conditions.
- Local people work together and with the police to reduce crime, drug addiction and gang activities.
- Charities work with street children and orphans to protect them from child poverty and abuse.

São Paulo's solutions

A number of schemes have been developed in São Paulo that have steadily brought about improvement to the poorest housing districts in the zone of the city called the periferia. Running water has been provided and main drains laid to dispose of waste water. Electricity was added to people's homes, and streetlights and improved roads provide a safer urban environment. This has been a slow, steady programme supported by the government and the local authority. Areas once lacking services now have a range of services such as schools, clinics and shops. This development encourages people to help themselves while providing support and advice to help them improve their own housing districts. It encourages businesses to set up, providing local jobs. Links are established to the city transport network to give access to the city centre and industrial areas.

Quick Test

1. What is a shantytown?
2. How does traffic have an effect on the quality of the environment in ELDCs?
3. Why does poor sanitation create problems in areas of cities in ELDCs?
4. For a city in an ELDC you have studied, briefly list the problems of the urban environment and match them to the solutions that have been tried.

Answers 1. An area of town that is unplanned and built by squatters from any material that comes to hand. **2.** Traffic causes poor air quality. **3.** Poor sanitation encourages water related diseases such as cholera, typhoid and diarrhoea. **4.** Answers could include: traffic – public transport; sanitation problems – water treatment and public water supply; shantytowns – self-help schemes.

Rural change in EMDCs 1

Farming systems in the EMDCs

Farming is a major industry in the developed countries and is referred to as **agribusiness**. From its original small scale of operation, farming now has to be able to respond rapidly to new developments in technology and government policy.

Top Tip
Use examples from your own visits to the supermarket or trips into the country to add to your answers. Personal experience counts.

Farming types in the European Union

Farms are referred to as extensive farms or intensive farms. These terms refer to the amount of work the farmers put into each unit of their land. **Extensive farms** are based on a large area with poorer land quality so the work on the farm is widespread to make it economic. **Hill farming**, raising sheep and beef cattle, fits into this category. Most of the available land is used for grazing as the harsh environmental conditions make growing crops difficult. **Intensive farms** make more money and are more likely to be growing crops in higher quantities and rearing animals in greater numbers. The amount of crop produced (**crop yield**) will be high per unit of land. Examples of this will be **arable farming** in the lowlands, **dairy farming**, **pig and poultry rearing** and **fruit and vegetable production**.

EU farming policies

The **European Union** lays down rules concerning the way farming operates so that farmers are working against a fair economic background. In this way, one member state of the EU cannot give its own farmers protection, and consumers across Europe are given an equal deal. EU guidance states that '*Farmers perform many different functions ranging from food and non-food agricultural products to countryside management, nature conservation, and tourism.*'

European agricultural policies

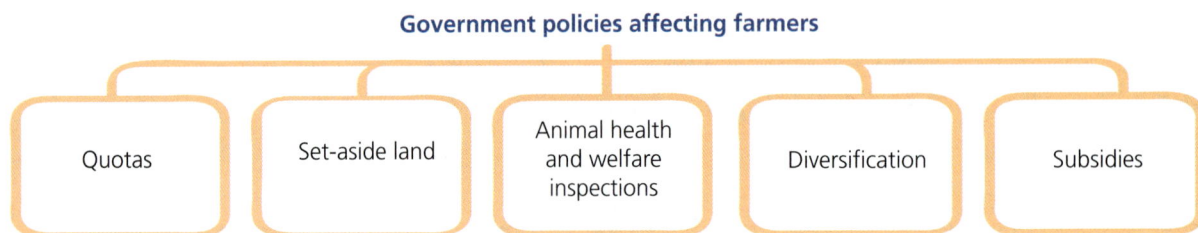

Government policies affecting farmers

| Quotas | Set-aside land | Animal health and welfare inspections | Diversification | Subsidies |

- **Set-aside** (land left unused by the farmer) has been used as a policy to prevent overproduction of crops and livestock.

- **Quotas** have been used in a similar way; this restricts the size of dairy herds and the amount of a crop grown in return for subsidies and guaranteed prices for products.

- **Animal health and welfare inspections** are used to ensure that farm animals are treated humanely and that this is the case for all EU members. Certain practices like the use of veal crates are banned.

- **Diversification** is encouraged so that farmers do not rely on a single product for their income but instead take part in a range of economic activities. This means that the farmer is less likely to be affected by a poor market in a particular product. Investment in other activities on the farm provides extra income and rural employment; it can also provide leisure and recreation opportunities and encourage environmental protection.

- **Subsidies** have been used by the EU in the past to make sure farmers had a stable income. Farmers were given guaranteed prices for their produce so that they did not suffer when prices at market were poor. This has changed to a new support system called single payment scheme.

Single payment scheme (SPS)

'The main aim of the single payment is to guarantee farmers more stable incomes. Farmers can decide what to produce in the knowledge that they will receive the same amount of aid, allowing them to adjust production to suit demand.'

Top Tip
Use satellite images from a program like Google Earth, Multimap or Windows Live Local to look for farm types and improve your understanding of this section. Start in your own local area.

Rural change in EMDCs 2

Changes on the farm

Changes on the farm: EU farm 1980

- ~~~ Hedges
- ▭ Fields
- ○ Trees
- ⌇ Gardens
- ▭ Main road
- ▬ Farm workers' cottages
- ▬ Farmhouse
- ▬ Stables
- ▬ Barn
- ▬ Dairy
- ▬ River

EU farm 2008

- — Hedges replaced by fences. This affects wildlife.
- ○ Trees
- ▭ Larger fields and more fertilisers used to boost crop yields.
- ▭ New road
- ▬ Holiday cottages
- ▬ Machinery shed
- ▬ Farm shop
- ▬ Extended farmhouse
- ▬ Dairy
- ○ Grain silos
- ▬ River
- ⊠ Holiday chalets
- ⬯ Fishing lake
- ▪▪▪▪ Flood protection bank

EU farm 1980: Pasture, Hay, Hay, Potatoes, Pasture cattle, Barley, Barley, Pasture, Hay, Oats, Pasture dairy cattle, Hay, Turnips, Barley

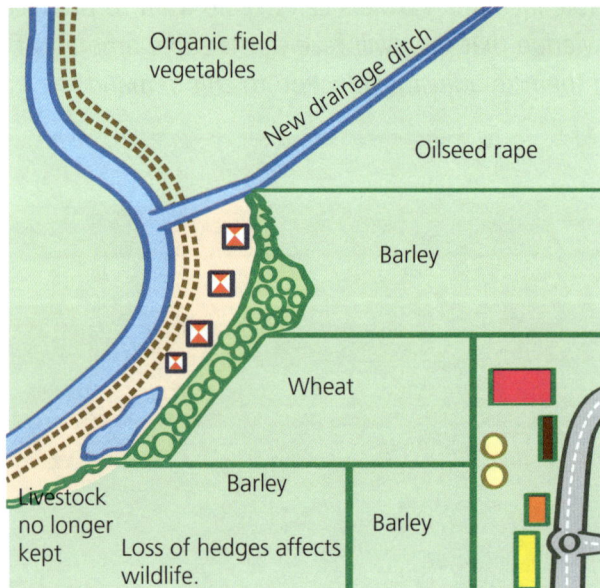

EU farm 2008: Organic field vegetables, New drainage ditch, Oilseed rape, Barley, Wheat, Barley, Livestock no longer kept, Loss of hedges affects wildlife, Barley

The diagrams show how a single EU farm has adapted itself to modern times. Farming is much more hi-tec and highly mechanised. Hedges have been removed to make larger fields, allowing larger machinery to be used. The farm specialises in high yield crops, using fertilisers and pesticides. Drainage and flood protection schemes have allowed increased production. Few animals are kept and the dairy no longer operates. Fewer people are now employed on the land. The farmer generates additional income by running a number of leisure, retail and tourist activities.

Changing settlement patterns in rural areas

Countryside areas are seeing changes in their settlement patterns for a number of reasons.

- Rural depopulation is taking place in remote areas and it is becoming increasingly difficult to keep services like village schools, post offices and small stores going as populations decline.

- People move into the countryside from large cities and commute to work. This can alter the character of villages as they become dormitory settlements.

- Distant town dwellers buy up houses in villages as holiday homes, leading to housing shortages for locals who cannot afford the high prices which wealthier town dwellers are able to pay.

- Fewer farm workers are employed so houses they once occupied are turned to other uses such as holiday lets.

- Villages on main roads are often affected by heavy traffic. A solution to this problem is the building of a bypass to protect the village and promote road safety.

- Commuter settlements grow around large towns and cities; villages may sprawl and lose their original character. Locals may not accept incomers.

Quick Test

1. Using examples, explain what is meant by intensive farming.

2. Give examples of extensive farming.

3. Explain, by providing examples, how technology has changed the way farmers operate their farms.

4. Why are fewer people employed on farms today than in the past?

Answers 1. High input, high yield farming such as intensive cereal growing or market gardening. **2.** Hill sheep farming or dry cereal farming in the Mediterranean region. **3.** Use of hi-tec machinery, irrigation systems and computer technology. **4.** More mechanisation; high cost of labour.

Rural change in ELDCs 1

Farming systems in the ELDCs

In economically less developed countries, ELDCs, farms tend to be smaller and are usually **family run units**. Small farms in developing countries are often **subsistence farms** where very little surplus is produced, so farm production goes to feed the farmer and his family. Small amounts of product may be sold at local markets to create extra income. Subsistence crops grown will be things like rice, vegetables, fruits, maize, millet, cassava, yams and sweet potatoes. Crops like cotton, tobacco, coffee and palm oil may be grown for sale as well.

Top Tip

Be sure to go over the particular case-study areas you covered in class. You might add some extra detail to the information here. Specific examples always score points.

Rural change in the ELDCs

Traditional peasant farming in the ELDCs is changing rapidly, encouraged by globalisation.

- Distant markets are more accessible due to air freight, railway, road developments, bulk shipping and refrigerated handling.

- There is increasing demand in rich consumer countries for certain food products in supermarkets.

- New technology allows mechanised working, improved irrigation and better fertilisers and pesticides.

- Government policies encourage the production of cash crops to generate income to boost GNP and to finance imports.

- Global corporations seek food resources like sugar, cocoa, fruit and vegetable oils in order to manufacture consumer products like chocolate bars and soft drinks.

The green revolution

This is a term used to describe the way scientific discoveries and new technologies have been applied to farming. This has had a major impact in the ELDCs.

- **High yield seeds** have been developed to produce bigger crops, for example, rice and wheat in India, among other places.
- **Genetically modified (GM) crops** are now being used with resistance to disease and drought. Adding the characteristics of one plant to another might adapt its colour, increase its growth rate or extend its shelf life.
- **New machinery** reduces labour costs and speeds up production.
- **Modern irrigation schemes** improve yields and allow up to three crops per year to be grown on the same land.

Problems linked to rural change in ELDCs

Development	Associated problem
High yield seeds	Suits large scale operations rather than small scale family farms. Requires expensive pesticides to control insect pests. Expensive fertilisers and the high cost of seeds impacts the farmers. The large companies involved in developing the seeds expect to make profits.
GM crops	May affect native crop varieties by cross-pollination. Government resistance to use and consumer resistance to products.
Hi-tec machinery	High cost, high maintenance, likely to cost jobs and out-compete small scale farmers in rural areas.
Modern irrigation	Using hi-tec methods involves high building and maintenance costs compared to traditional methods. Can lead to salt contamination if not used appropriately in dry areas. Multi cropping requires high inputs of fertiliser or land becomes exhausted.

Quick Test

1. What is meant by the term subsistence farming?
2. Why do farmers rely on markets?
3. What modern developments affect farming in ELDCs?
4. How can technology help farmers?
5. What does sustainability mean?

Answers 1. Farming to produce for the family only and not for sale for profit. **2.** To sell their goods and to get a good price for products. Also to buy seed and livestock. **3.** Irrigation systems, new varieties of crops. **4.** Modern machinery helps farmers to produce more. Chemical fertilisers and pesticides improve farming production. **5.** The ability of a farming system to keep going year after year without damaging the environment.

Rural change in ELDCs 2

Population change in rural areas of ELDCs

Rural areas in developing countries continue to experience population growth, which puts pressure on land and water resources. Larger farm units are created by the wealthy few and by large companies. High levels of debt may be a problem as farmers try to modernise and develop their farms. This can lead to people losing their land or being unable to buy land to work. Landless people find only low-paid work, educational achievement is likely to be low and **rural poverty** may be the result. This is likely to lead to **migration** in search of a better life in towns and cities.

Migration explained

Why do people migrate?

Urban pull
Better job opportunities
Higher potential earnings
Better health and education services
Better amenities and infrastructure

Rural push
Poor job opportunities, low pay
Poor health and education services
Less access to service and industrial jobs

In reality the high hopes people have of a better life in the city may not be realised. Instead they may be forced to endure the poor living conditions experienced in the shantytowns they find themselves in. Population numbers fed by migration from the countryside and rapid industrialisation have led to **urban sprawl**. This can quickly swallow up productive agricultural land on the edge of cities. Farmers bordering the city can have their crops damaged by polluted air and water or raided by hungry people. Livestock may be stolen or may stray into town among traffic. Firewood gathering, for example, around villages and towns in the Sahel in West Africa, can lead to land drying out and soil being eroded. Urban dwellers may keep cattle in the surrounding countryside which is likely to lead to problems of overgrazing and desertification.

The impact of tourism on rural areas

Tourism provides extra income to rural communities in ELDCs.

- New markets for farm produce are opened up in order to provide produce for hotels and restaurants. Large numbers of tourists visit Kenya for beach and safari holidays.

- Tourists buy products in local markets such as fruit and fish.

- Tourists visit National Parks like the Masai Mara in Kenya, providing income for the Masai farmers who are able to sell souvenirs and provide cultural experiences for the visitors.

- Wildlife is protected but eco-tourism replaces the income lost when hunting is banned.

Quick Test

1. What is the green revolution?

2. How does urban sprawl affect farmers?

3. For a rural area you have studied, describe the impact tourism has had on the people living there.

Answers 1. The development of hi-tec farming methods that allow improvements in crop and livestock production such as high-yield crop varieties. **2.** Urban areas encroach on nearby farmlands and affect their viability. Crops can be trampled and livestock affected by people living nearby. Land prices can become higher as housing and industry take up more and more land. **3.** Answer could include: tourism can allow farmers to diversify into holiday lets and things like outdoor pursuits.

Industrial change 1

The changing industrial scene

Industrial location is dynamic which means that it is constantly changing. There are a number of reasons why industry locates to particular places and why it then grows or eventually closes down.

Why industry comes and goes

Reasons for the changing location of industry

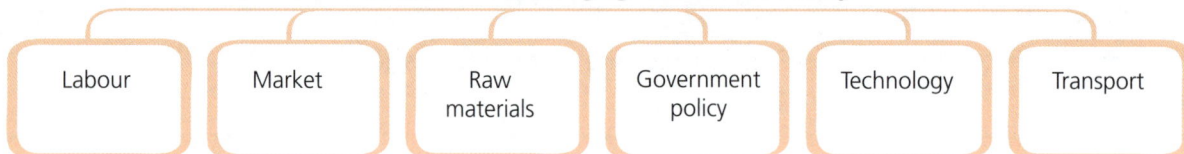

Labour	Market	Raw materials	Government policy	Technology	Transport

Heavy industrial landscape

Mines close down when they become too expensive to work or the coal runs out.

Stone is quarried for cement and building.

Farmland provides raw materials such as wool and timber.

Power stations need fuel: coal, oil, gas, nuclear fuel. They also need water for cooling.

Mining town – relies on the mine

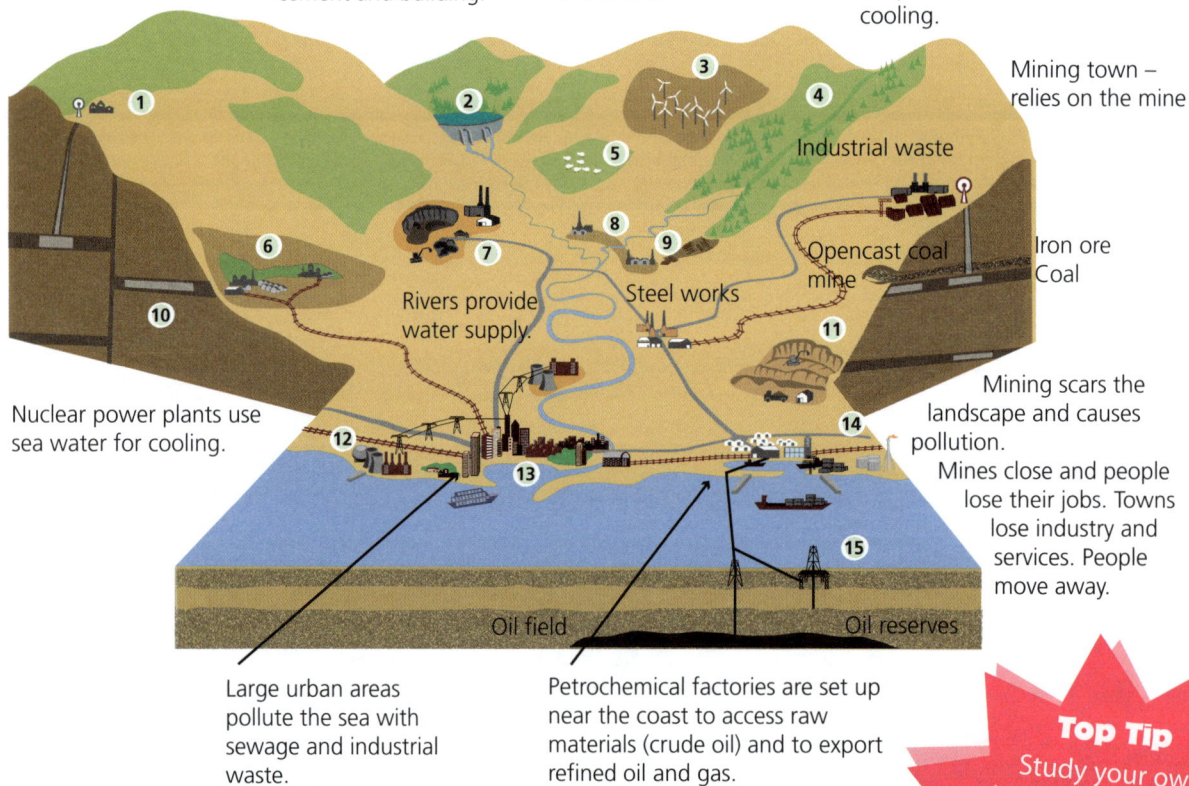

Industrial waste

Iron ore
Coal

Rivers provide water supply.

Steel works

Opencast coal mine

Mining scars the landscape and causes pollution.

Nuclear power plants use sea water for cooling.

Mines close and people lose their jobs. Towns lose industry and services. People move away.

Oil field

Oil reserves

Large urban areas pollute the sea with sewage and industrial waste.

Petrochemical factories are set up near the coast to access raw materials (crude oil) and to export refined oil and gas.

1. Mining village
2. Reservoir for water supply and hydroelectric power (HEP)
3. Wind farm: renewable energy
4. Forestry
5. Sheep farming: wool
6. Mining town – relies on the mine
7. Cement works and limestone quarry
8. Textile mills
9. Paper mill
10. Coal reserves
11. Opencast coal mine
12. Nuclear power plant
13. Major port
14. Oil refinery
15. Oil production platforms

Top Tip
Study your own home area and look at industrial sites with an eye to suggesting why the industry set up where it did.

- **Raw materials** – industry often sets up near its source of raw material because it can be expensive to transport materials to the processing plant. In this way industry grows near sources of power such as coal, oil or gas and next to the materials it needs like mineral ores, e.g. iron or copper ore. Industries may use large amounts of water so nearby water resources may be important.

- **Labour** – this will be required by factories and industrial plants to operate the works and machinery. People working in industries need to have skills. The cost of labour will vary but there is a general rule that the higher the skill level, the higher the cost of labour. Labour can be moved to new sites or can be replaced by cheaper labour elsewhere.

- **Transport** – over long distances transport is expensive, so the cost of moving goods to and from the factory needs to be kept as low as possible to make a profit. Industry often sets up next to railways, navigable rivers, canals, sea ports and motorways to move goods as quickly and as cheaply as possible. Air freight is expensive but may be used to transport high value goods such as medical supplies or perishable products with a short shelf life.

- **Technology** – new developments change the types of industry that exist and how industry produces goods for sale. New technology replaces old methods of production, making old factories inefficient and unable to compete. Hi-tec industry is less tied to raw materials and is called **footloose industry** as it can set up in many locations.

- **Market** – industry relies on buying and selling goods so it needs to have good markets for buying raw materials and for selling its finished products. Prices on world markets change and can make an industrial plant so uneconomic it will close down. The market for goods can change as one product replaces another. For example, electricity replaced coal power and man made fibres replaced wool for making clothing.

- **Government policy** – industry provides jobs and money for the economy so it is natural for governments to put policies in place to help and develop industry. Grants, tax incentives and subsidies are used to support existing industries and to protect them against foreign competition. They also encourage investors to set up new industrial sites.

Top Tip
To find industrial areas on a map look for main roads, railways and waterways.

Quick Test

1. Study the Middlesbrough OS map on page 62 and suggest the sort of raw materials likely to be used by the industrial areas shown.

2. List the forms of transport that can be found on the map.

3. Why did the government provide money to redevelop areas shown on the Middlesbrough map?

Answers 1. Coal, iron ore, oil and chemicals. **2.** Shipping, rail, road, canal and air. **3.** The area saw old industries like the steel industry and coal mining decline so newer petrochemical industries and light manufacturing were encouraged to set up here to provide jobs and a boost to the economy.

Industrial change 2

Changing landscapes

Middlesbrough is a typical industrial town in the north of England. It sits on the south bank of the River Tees, where the river meets the sea at its estuary. This has allowed Middlesbrough to develop as a port and to become a major industrial centre. The Middlesbrough OS map reveals many of the features typical of old-established industrial areas, as well as those typical of modern technological industry (petrochemicals) and shows typical modern industries found on smaller industrial estates in the UK.

Changing industrial location

- Older industrial areas developed in the nineteenth century based on heavy industry such as engineering and shipbuilding. These areas were often close to the city centre and near to docks, for importing and exporting raw materials and finished goods. They relied on coal power for energy and needed to be close to railway networks to move goods and materials. Labour supply lived nearby in rows of terraced houses. Grid squares 4821 and 4921 show industrial docklands of this type. Typical working-class housing in the inner city can be seen close by in square 4819.

- Change and redevelopment is likely to take place in areas like this as old docks fall into disuse. Old industrial buildings became derelict as industries like shipbuilding closed down and finally disappeared in the 1970s and 1980s. Ships have become larger so port developments have moved to deeper water downstream. Deep-water port facilities can be seen at Teesport in square 5423.

- Modern technological industry can be seen on the flat floodplains to the north-east of Middlesbrough. Large steelworks can be seen in square 5521 and chemical works relying on supplies of North Sea oil and gas are located nearby in square 5621. Labour supply no longer lives next to the plant but is more likely to commute to work by road or railway using local stations like the one at 533213. Large power stations like the one at 564203 provide the electricity that modern industry relies on. Heavy industry and power plants still rely on nearby water supply from rivers like the Tees for their processes.

- Modern industrial estates depend on good road networks for transporting goods and raw materials. A typical pattern for this land use can be found at 5220 and 5219. The large blocks of buildings shown indicate industrial use. A good indication of road access is given by the roundabouts on the nearby roads. Out-of-town industrial estates can be seen in square 5316. Again, note the nearby modern road network.

Infrastructure

Infrastructure refers to transport and communications networks that connect people, places and industrial areas to ports, markets, resources and other areas.

Infrastructure feature	Purpose	OS map characteristics
Port facilities	Handling incoming and outgoing goods. Raw materials like metal ores, oil and chemical feed stocks are imported. Older facilities are down river on shallow water. Newer port facilities are located next to deep water and can handle larger bulk carrier ships with special machinery.	Look for large industrial sites on flat ground away from housing and town centres. Note the access to land transport routes. Teesport 5423
Railways	Moving heavy goods and raw materials to industrial plants and carrying finished products to customers and markets. Important to old and new heavy industry for moving bulky goods at speed.	Pick out main line tracks on the map. Connection to industrial plants relies on the smaller 'mineral' lines to connect industrial plants to the main line. 540218 is a typical branch line direct into an ore or coal stock yard.
Roads	Roads carry much of Britain's industrial traffic. Major roads have multiple carriageways to accomodate large volumes of traffic and heavy lorries. Redevelopment of old industrial sites in the 1970s and 1980s allowed the building of these roads through major urban areas like Middlesbrough.	Look out for the blue motorways on other maps and the wide red dual carriageways seen on the Middlesbrough map at 504200. Patterns to look for are roundabouts that speed traffic movement, 'spaghetti junctions' (4819), and flyovers.
Power lines	Carry electricity and, increasingly, telecommunications.	Note the symbol for these in the OS key; find them in the vicinity of power stations 5620.
Airports	Carry workers to oilfields offshore and air freight such as biomedical products that require fast or secure delivery.	Normally well clear of urban areas for safety reasons but likely be near to industrial estates. Will be well served by road networks, rail links and tramways.

Quick Test

1. Why did older industrial plants rely on railways?

2. Why have ports and docks moved to deeper water in recent years?

3. Why do modern industrial plants set up on the outside of towns and cities rather than in the city centre?

Answers 1. Railways helped move heavy raw materials and finished products to and from sources and markets. **2.** Ships have got bigger. **3.** There is more space and less traffic congestion and these areas link into modern transport systems.

Environmental Interactions: Unit outcomes

In the third unit of the Intermediate 2 Geography course you are given a **choice** of study topics. You must complete a course of study in **two** out of a total of five topics.
- **Rural land degradation**
- **River basin management**
- **European environmental inequalities**
- **Development and health**
- **Environmental hazards**

Top Tip
Be sure to check which of the optional questions you have studied and know where they occur in section B of the exam

Case-studies

This unit relies on **case-studies** that your teacher or tutor will have picked and you should be aware of these as you use this *Success Guide*. It is unlikely that this book will deal with your particular case-studies as these could be taken from anywhere. This book does try to identify the basic principles behind the issues in the unit, however, and to give some specific case-study examples, but these are **not** designed to replace your own case-studies. It also gives you some ideas on how to approach problem solving questions in the exam paper and suggests a way of analysing past paper questions.

Skills

In completing this and other units you will have developed your writing skills and you will have been able to use a range of sources such as written sources, maps and graphics. You will have also learned how to use notes and audiovisual sources. In revision you can continue to use some of these to build up and improve your case-studies. You will now be familiar with a good range of geographical terms and concepts. Work completed in other units of the course can be applied to the optional units you study. For example, in Environmental interactions, work done on river landscapes in Physical Environments links well with river basin management. The development and health and environmental hazards options link into Unit 2: Human Environments, with its work on population studies. In the exam it is important that you use the resources provided on the paper, such as maps and diagrams, as well as the detail you have taken from the course. The key to success in this unit is understanding the interrelationships between the physical and human worlds.

Unit skills

- Using a variety of maps
- Completing and analysing choropleth, isoline, proportional symbol and topological maps
- Using and completing graphs: bar, line, scatter, pie

Rural land degradation

Rural land degradation happens when people use the land in such a way that it produces less or stops producing altogether. This section uses a world context but does not include examples from the British Isles. It involves either forest **destruction** or **desertification** in arid (desert) or semi-arid areas. Land degradation has effects on the landscape, the environment and on people living in the area affected. You should refer to your class case-studies here.

The causes and effects of land degradation

Land degradation is usually the result of population pressure on the land. Too many people trying to squeeze a living out of too little land takes the soil beyond its ability to maintain itself. Soils, over-cropped, over-grazed and without vegetation, rapidly break down and become eroded by water or blown away as they dry out.

Forest destruction

Poor people desperate for land clear large areas of forest. The diagram shows how this can affect people living hundreds of kilometres downstream by causing flooding. In **Amazonia** forest clearance for farming, timber and mining damages **habitats for wildlife** and displaces native peoples. Squatters clear forest and conflict with others such as indigenous peoples or cattle ranchers.

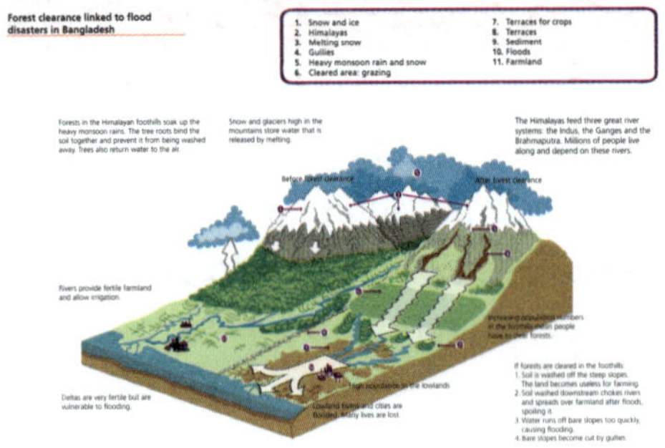

Forest clearance linked to flood disasters in Bangladesh

1. Snow and ice	7. Terraces for crops
2. Himalayan	8. Terraces
3. Melting snow	9. Sediment
4. Gullies	10. Floods
5. Heavy monsoon rain and snow	11. Farmland
6. Cleared area: grazing	

See larger version on www.leckieandleckie.co.uk.

Desertification

Desertification takes place on the edges of deserts such as the Sahara, where land that can be used for farming is overused and becomes like desert as it degrades. In this way it goes out of economic production.

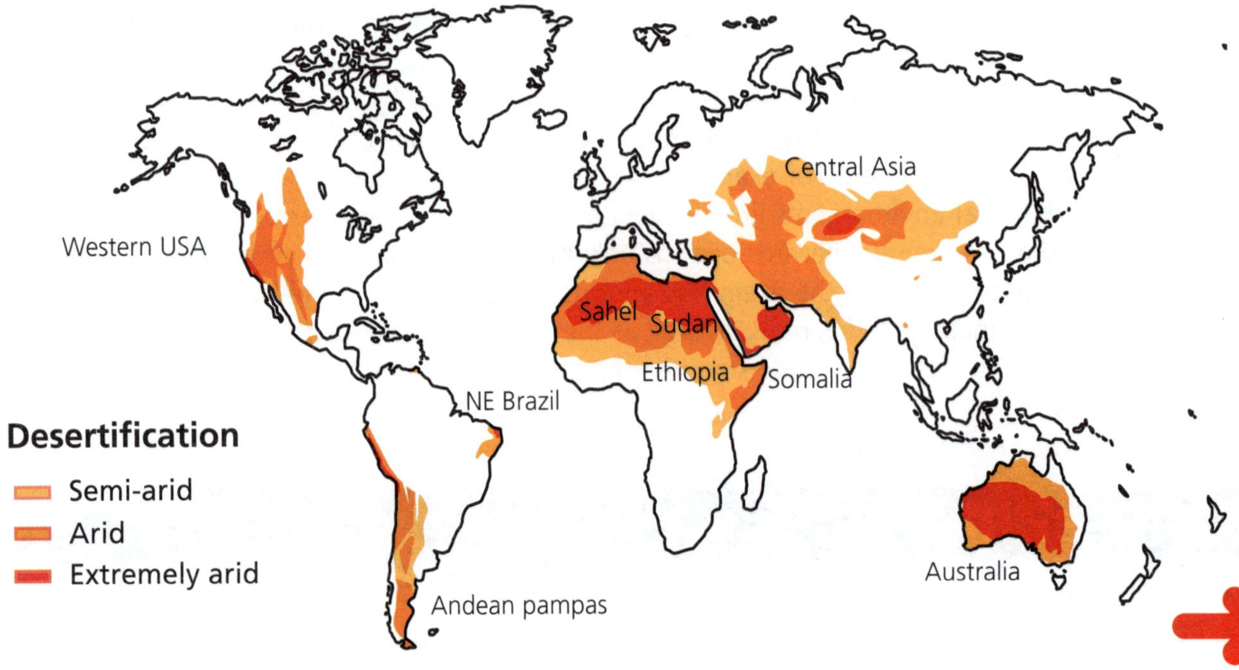

Desertification

- Semi-arid
- Arid
- Extremely arid

Western USA

Central Asia

Sahel Sudan

Ethiopia Somalia

NE Brazil

Australia

Andean pampas

➡️ The main causes of desertification are **increasing population** numbers, **changing farming systems** that exclude people from open grazing land and **global climate change** which causes **drought**.

- Woodlands and forests are cleared for firewood around towns and villages.

- Overgrazing by too many cattle, sheep or goats leaves the land bare of vegetation. Topsoil blows away or is washed away in the rainy season.

- Climate change caused by global warming, or local environment change means droughts occur more often and are more severe.

- High population growth puts too much pressure on the land.

- Poor irrigation methods mean that salt is left behind as water evaporates from farmland (**salinisation**) so crops can't grow.

Managing land resources to prevent land degradation

The diagram below gives some of the problems and solutions associated with land degradation in forest and desert environments.

Dealing with land degradation

1. Land fenced to prevent overgrazing by animals.
2. Erosion dams prevent soil being washed downstream.
3. Lines of stones (stone stripes) prevent soil erosion on slopes.
4. Contour ploughing prevents soil being washed downhill. Terraces have the same effect.
5. Dams control floods and provide hydro power and irrigation water.
6. Forest planting protects the soil, reduces flooding. Firebreaks and watchtowers prevent fires.
7. Environmental monitoring warns of problems.
8. Flood banks and drains control flooding.
9. Electric power stations reduce the use of forests for fuel.
10. Shelterbelts (tree-lined fields) are used to prevent wind erosion.
11. Flood protection schemes protect the coast.
12. Birth control checks population growth.
13. Tourism and industrial development provides new jobs and relieves population pressures.
14. Solar panels provide renewable power, reducing CO_2 emissions.
15. Modern irrigation methods such as booms and drip feeds reduce the risk of salinisation.

Forest clearance problem

Desertification problem

Oasis

Sustainable land use means that resources are managed effectively without destroying them so that they are protected for the future.

See larger version on www.leckieandleckie.co.uk.

Quick Test

1. What are the main processes involved in soil erosion?

2. What is overgrazing and how does it affect the soil?

3. Why does salinisation occur when areas are irrigated?

Answers 1. Such things as forest clearance and overgrazing that expose the bare soil to erosion by wind and running water. **2.** Overgrazing is when livestock such as sheep, cattle and goats eat vegetation like grass beyond the point from which it will recover. **3.** Salinisation occurs because the water table comes too near the surface and ground water is evaporated leaving salt deposits building up in the top soil.

Case-study 1: Amazon rainforest clearance

The destruction of rainforest in Amazonia is a commonly used example of rural land degradation.

Physical environment

Climate

The Amazon rainforest is dominated by an equatorial climate which has average temperatures of 26 degrees Celsius in each month of the year due to its location on or close to the equator. Rainfall is heavy, with over 2000 mm of rain per month and rainfall totals in excess of 10 000 mm, making this one of the wettest places on Earth.

Soils and vegetation

Deep soils appear more fertile than they really are. The dense vegetation, layers of understory young trees and shrubs, the canopy of tree crowns and giant trees that break out above the canopy suggest that things grow quickly and easily here.

- Soil fertility is found in the upper part of the soil.
- Dead and decaying plant material is quickly recycled in the forest system.
- Trees have shallow, widespread roots to access nutrients near the ground surface.
- Soils are leached of their nutrients by rainwater washing them down through the soil, thus removing soil fertility.

Relief

Amazonia is criss-crossed by large tributaries that flow into the Amazon which then flows on to the Atlantic. Rivers cut into the landscape creating steep valleys, making this challenging terrain to travel over, farm, industrialise or to settle on.

Top Tip
Bullet words hit the target and score points. Use words like *leaching, gullying, dust bowl, sustainable development.*

Human environment

Population density is low because the land does not support large numbers of people without being degraded. Amazon Indians live in the rainforest in tribal groups. Examples are the Wai Wai and the Sanema peoples. They live by **hunting** (wild animals), **gathering** (forest foods) and **shifting cultivation** (slash and burn agriculture).

Indian farmers use slash and burn to clear 'garden' plots by cutting vegetation down and burning it to provide ash fertiliser. The land is farmed for between three and twelve years, growing crops like

Top Tip
Examples of peoples and the crops they grow is an effective way to score marks if used correctly.

manioc, yams, bananas, maize, sweet potatoes and tobacco. The bare soil is leached by the heavy rainfall and gradually becomes infertile. People move on to another part of the rainforest and start the process again. The soils and vegetation recover on the original plot so the forest re-establishes. Therefore this is a **sustainable lifestyle**.

Causes of degradation

There are a number of causes of land degradation

- New roads such as the Trans Amazon Highway allow new people to move into the area.

- People are encouraged to take up farming in the area but find it difficult to make a living on small plots of land. Some are forced into unsustainable forms of shifting cultivation and the land becomes exhausted to the point that the soil does not recover. The land is degraded by soil erosion and gullying.

- Large cattle ranches burn large areas of forest to produce beef cattle for distant urban markets.

- Forests are cleared for timber.

- Mining clears forests and contaminates rivers.

Managing the development of Amazonia

The Brazilian Government recognises the economic importance of Amazonia but also tries to protect its indigenous peoples. National Parks and forest reserves have been created to try to conserve areas of the forest in the long term. Funding, from aid givers such as the World Bank, attempts to encourage sustainable projects. Similarly, consumers in rich countries are encouraged to buy timber from branded sustainable sources. Managed felling of forests provides replacement trees. Illegal mining is discouraged and mining companies are required to plan to avoid contamination of water by building settling tanks for mine waste. Hydraulic mining techniques that leave land damaged are avoided or restricted.

Quick Test

Bearing in mind the detail given in the case-study above, develop a bullet point answer plan for the following questions:

1. For the forest area you have studied describe the physical environmental conditions.

2. Describe the human environment of your area.

3. List the main causes of land degradation linked to deforestation in your study area.

4. Explain the ways in which people have attempted to control degradation.

Answers 1. Possible descriptive terms will be: hot, humid, equatorial forest, av. temp 26 degrees Celsius, over 2000 mm rainfall, canopy, emergents, understory. **2.** Descriptive terms will refer to difficult terrain, land cut by rivers, dense vegetation, isolated settlements, communications difficulties, transport by rivers. **3.** Forest clearance for cattle ranching, for timber resources, for major building projects such as dams and roads, for providing land for squatter farmers under slash and burn farming. **4.** By creating national parks and forest reserves, by buying areas of rainforest for conservation purposes, by buying only from sustainable forest sources in shops.

Case-study 2: the Sahel

Physical environment

Climate

The Sahel is a zone of semi-arid land lying to the south of the Sahara Desert. Some of the poorest of the ELDCs are contained in this area, such as Sudan, Ethiopia and Somalia.

Deserts receive under 250 mm of rainfall per year. The Sahel gets more than this but rain falls for just a few months per year. Much of the year the Sahel is dry and if the rains fail then drought occurs, sometimes year after year.

Soil, vegetation and landscape

Soils in the Sahel support sparse vegetation such as short grasses. Trees grow where ground water is available. The wet season sees lots of greenery. Nomadic peoples like the Tuareg and the Fulani of West Africa graze herds of cattle, sheep, goats or camels in the Sahel. The landscape varies with rolling plains, valleys with seasonal rivers, rocky mountains and sand dunes.

Human environment

Population density

Population density is low with high birth rates and growing urban population. This is putting pressure on the land.

Farming systems

Farming relies on the seasonal rainfall providing water for crops such as millet, maize, ground nuts and a range of vegetables such as sweet potatoes. Villagers cultivate gardens and tend herds of grazing animals. Nomads follow the rains, moving herds long distances in search of grazing and water holes. Reliable sources of water such as oases provide ideal growing conditions for a range of fruit and vegetables such as dates, potatoes, tomatoes and field vegetables such as beans. Crops are grown to sell locally or just to support the family (subsistence).

Modern irrigation schemes have dammed across rivers such as the Niger in West Africa and crops like rice and cotton can be grown for cash.

Causes of degradation: desertification

- Poor irrigation control raises the water table too close to the surface. Water evaporates from the soil and leave salt behind in the soil. This is called salinisation and it damages the soil and makes it unproductive and desert-like.

- Increasing population leads to overgrazing, meaning grasses are eaten beyond the point of recovery. This leaves bare exposed soil which can be blown (dust bowl conditions) or washed away when the rains come. Damaged soils become unable to support farming, making the land desert-like.

- Disruption due to civil war in countries like Somalia and Sudan forces people to migrate, causing conflict with people who already occupy the land.

- Urbanisation leads to pressure on the land as townsfolk keep cattle nearby. Overgrazing and firewood gathering from the surrounding countryside destroy woodland that protects soil.

- Global warming and climate change caused by vegetation change reduces rainfall, helping the Sahara to extend into the Sahel.

Effects of degradation

Desertification reduces the ability of the land to support farming families. Civil war and environmental change cause disruption of populations in Sudan, Ethiopia and Somalia. Drought leads to famines across the Sahel where as many as 30 million people are affected by desertification. Famine resulted in the Band Aid, Live Aid and Comic Relief charity events in the 1980s and beyond.

Managing the problem

The following courses of action may help to avoid or reduce the effects of desertification.

- Placing stones and low walls around fields (stone stripes) to prevent soil erosion by wind and water.

- Building dams across gullies prevents soil erosion.

- Planting fast-growing gum trees provides firewood and shelter belts against wind erosion. Shelter crops and bushes are planted between rows of low-growing crops.

- Using more efficient irrigation systems (rotating boom sprinklers or drip feeds) prevents salinisation.

- Contour ploughing prevents soils washing down steep slopes.

- Agencies provide emergency food aid during famines and advice to farmers on conservation and land management techniques.

- Encouraging birth control reduces population growth.

- Proper fencing can prevent overgrazing.

- Employing peacekeepers to end civil wars.

Many of these measures have proved effective but civil war rages on and, in the short term, global warming is out of the control of the nations involved. Populations continue to grow and urban areas continue to spread.

Quick Test

1. What is a desert?

2. What is salinisation?

3. How does a charity event like Comic Relief help areas undergoing desertification?

Answers 1. An area with less than 250 mm of rainfall per year. **2.** The process by which land and water become too salty to use. **3.** It can help by providing such things as wells and expert advice that creates sustainable farming.

River basin management

The water cycle and river basins

This unit involves the study of river basins outside Europe, looking at river basins as systems involving inputs, processes and outputs. How people interfere with these systems causes change with both positive and negative consequences. You will have studied a case-study river basin in detail.

Global hydrological cycle

Hydrological (water) cycle

A. Evaporation from the ocean
B. Condensation: cloud formas
C. Precipitation: rain falls
D. Some water is stored in lakes and in rocks and soil.
E. Rivers return water to the ocean.

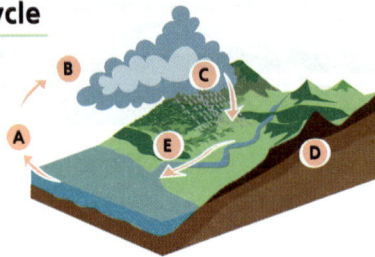

River basin system

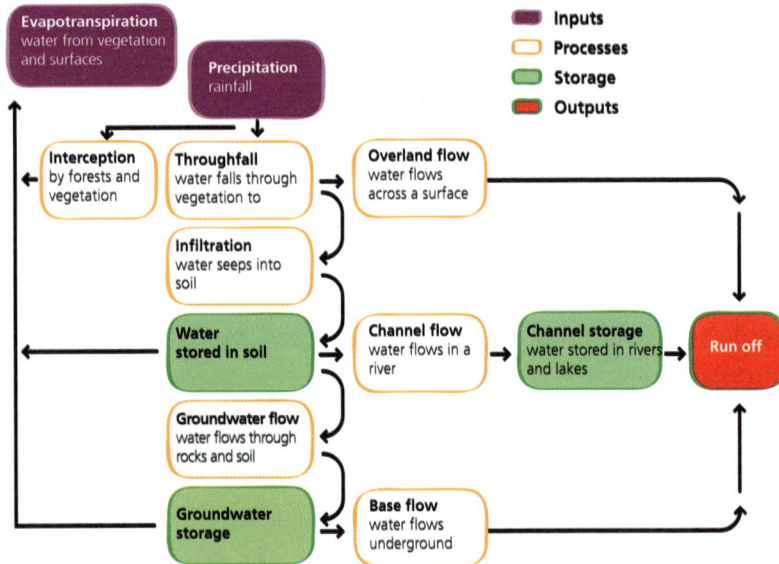

Legend:
- Inputs
- Processes
- Storage
- Outputs

Evapotranspiration water from vegetation and surfaces

Precipitation rainfall

Interception by forests and vegetation

Throughfall water falls through vegetation to

Overland flow water flows across a surface

Infiltration water seeps into soil

Water stored in soil

Channel flow water flows in a river

Channel storage water stored in rivers and lakes

Run off

Groundwater flow water flows through rocks and soil

Groundwater storage

Base flow water flows underground

Top Tip
Some questions take the form of problem solving exercises. When dealing with these you need to apply the knowledge you have gained during the course to a new situation to work out the solution to the problem.

A river basin is an area through which a river and all its tributaries drain. It is contained within a watershed which separates it from all other river basins. River basins may be small in the case of a local river but may involve vast areas such as the Mississippi or Nile basins.

- The bigger the basin the greater the effects of climate, such as distant rainfall in high mountains, seasonal rains, melting snow in spring.
- The bigger the basin the greater the effects of geology and landscapes.
- The bigger the basin the greater the variety of land and water uses – domestic water supply, industry, farming, transport, leisure and recreation, energy production.

Problem solving – a model river basin

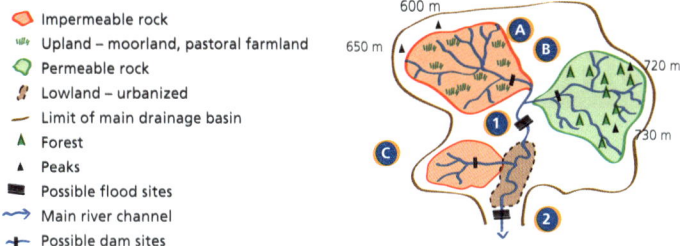

Look at the model river basin, read the questions and think about the possible solutions given to the problem below.

Problem-solving: a model river basin

- Impermeable rock
- Upland – moorland, pastoral farmland
- Permeable rock
- Lowland – urbanized
- Limit of main drainage basin
- Forest
- Peaks
- Possible flood sites
- Main river channel
- Possible dam sites

See larger version on www.leckieandleckie.co.uk.

Problem solving question 1

The model river basin diagram above shows three possible sites for a new dam. Which site would be the most suitable for a river basin management scheme? Give reasons for your answer. **(4 marks)**

	Possible dam site: reasons for	Possible dam site: reasons against
Dam site A	**Impermeable rock** ideal for building storage reservoirs. Upland moorland has no forest cover so **run-off will be rapid** from this area. The dam will be an ideal flood control measure. Dam and reservoir will have less **environmental impact** on an area of grazing.	Farmers would object to losing their farm land. Lower lying land gets lower rainfall.
Dam site B	Higher ground than other areas proposed, so more rain/snow likely to fall here. Could be effective in controlling floods. **Like site A** this has many river tributaries contributing to the overall flow of the river. Both control flooding at points 1 and 2.	**Permeable rock** allows water to seep through it so is poor for building storage reservoirs. Extensive forest here already **controls flooding** by slowing down water entering the river system by interception. High level of **environmental impact** as reservoirs will disrupt wildlife and natural systems in the forested landscape.
Dam site C	Close to the urbanised land, allows the area to be used for recreation.	Too small to have a major impact on the river. Only controls flooding in the lower basin.

Solution

Aiming the answer towards dam site A is the best choice although there are arguments for B as well. Site C is difficult to argue a case for.

Problem solving question 2

'Surface features can affect run-off.'

If there was a prolonged period of heavy rainfall, which of the two points 1 or 2 on the river is most likely to flood? Give reasons for your answer. **(4 marks)**

Potential flood point

Point 1	Point 2
Lack of forest in area A will cause rapid run-off but the storage by forest in area B will control it. The permeable rock also acts as a natural water store slowing run-off. Higher up the river valley is less likely to flood.	This point is the most vulnerable to flooding as it gets rapid run-off from the two un-forested, impermeable rock basins plus additional input from area B. The urban area is also likely to cause rapid run-off due to man-made impermeable surfaces and flood control measures set up by the city. Wide meanders suggest a wide vulnerable flood plain.

Solution

Point 2 has the highest flood risk and is the easiest case to argue.

River basin management: conflicts

Conflicts in a river basin

Large numbers of people use the land and water resources in a river basin. The diagram below shows conflicts that can occur along a river and its tributaries, as well as the solutions to some of these problems.

Top Tip
Use the diagram to identify the issues that have been detailed in your case-study area.

Unregulated river basins – causes and effects of river basin problems

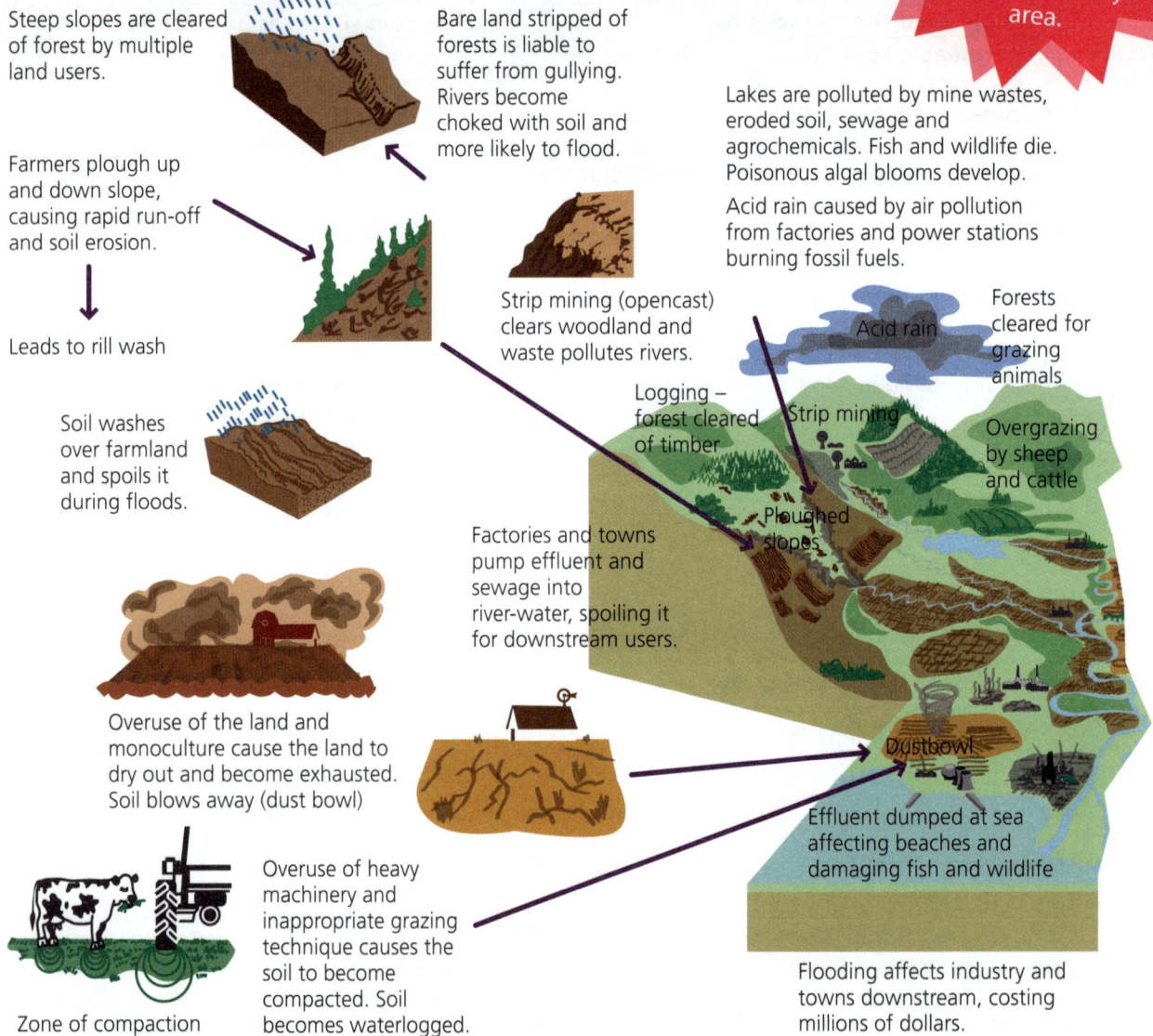

Steep slopes are cleared of forest by multiple land users.

Bare land stripped of forests is liable to suffer from gullying. Rivers become choked with soil and more likely to flood.

Lakes are polluted by mine wastes, eroded soil, sewage and agrochemicals. Fish and wildlife die. Poisonous algal blooms develop.

Acid rain caused by air pollution from factories and power stations burning fossil fuels.

Farmers plough up and down slope, causing rapid run-off and soil erosion.

Leads to rill wash

Strip mining (opencast) clears woodland and waste pollutes rivers.

Soil washes over farmland and spoils it during floods.

Logging – forest cleared of timber

Factories and towns pump effluent and sewage into river-water, spoiling it for downstream users.

Acid rain

Strip mining

Forests cleared for grazing animals

Overgrazing by sheep and cattle

Ploughed slopes

Dustbowl

Overuse of the land and monoculture cause the land to dry out and become exhausted. Soil blows away (dust bowl)

Overuse of heavy machinery and inappropriate grazing technique causes the soil to become compacted. Soil becomes waterlogged.

Zone of compaction

Effluent dumped at sea affecting beaches and damaging fish and wildlife

Flooding affects industry and towns downstream, costing millions of dollars.

Your case-study will involve a water management project. These are often called multipurpose river basin development schemes. These schemes may be organised across states in a single country (the Tennessee Valley Authority – TVA – in the USA) or across international boundaries (the River Nile in Egypt, Sudan and Ethiopia). The key point is that what one person does with the land or water of the river has a knock on effect for people downstream. Water control projects help people get the most from water resources without destroying the environment and affecting other users in a negative way.

Regulated river basins – potential solutions of river basin problems

Clean water-courses, lakes and rivers, abundant wildlife, healthy ecosystems

Fences control grazing

Watershed or drainage

Renewable energy reduces acid rain.

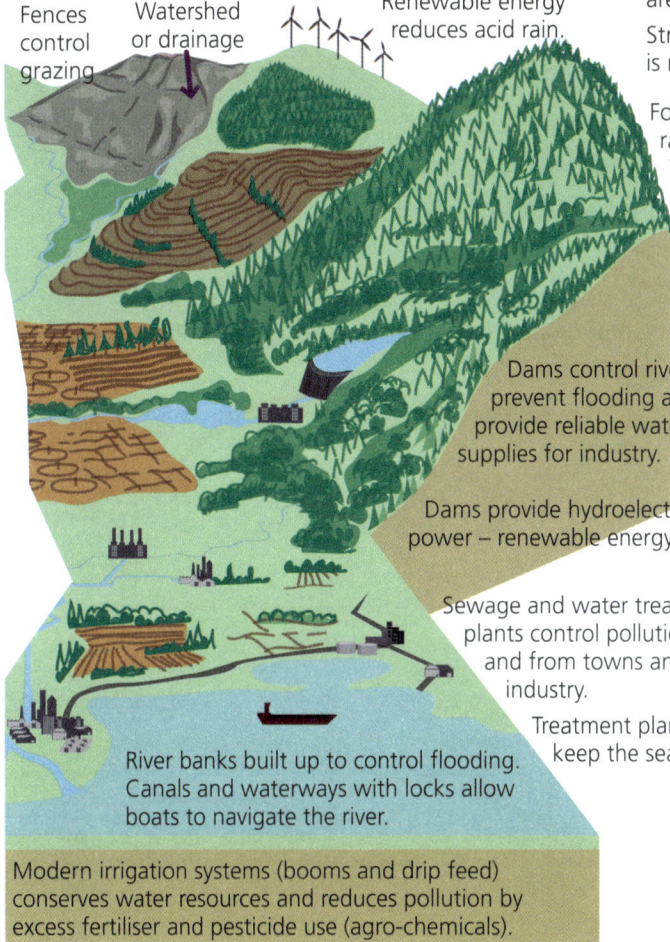

Nature and wildlife is encouraged. People use the forests and waterside areas for recreation and tourism. Many jobs are provided.

Strip mining is controlled. Land is restored after the resource is removed. Strict controls on pollution entering the river.

Forests are managed rather than clear-felled. Trees bind the soil with their roots and so control run-off.

Contour ploughing to reduce soil erosion and flooding.

Dams control river-flow, prevent flooding and provide reliable water supplies for industry.

Modern power plants burn coal or oil but have reduced emissions (due to chimney scrubbers).

Dams provide hydroelectric power – renewable energy.

New roads provide fast, efficient communication.

Sewage and water treatment plants control pollution to and from towns and industry.

Treatment plants keep the sea clean.

Barriers in plough furrows stop soil erosion due to rapid run-off.

Barrier

River banks built up to control flooding. Canals and waterways with locks allow boats to navigate the river.

Modern irrigation systems (booms and drip feed) conserves water resources and reduces pollution by excess fertiliser and pesticide use (agro-chemicals).

Tied ridge

- Social effects see people getting jobs, improved living conditions and opportunities for improved leisure and recreation.

- Economic effects see higher levels of production and improvements in farming, power generation potential, industrial development and transport (increased river traffic), both locally and nationally.

- Political effects mean people are more settled and suffer less economic and social hardship. This creates political stability and improves backward regions which may be lacking development.

- Environmental effects lead to sustainable development that also helps wildlife and nature conservation. Water control projects also provide recreational areas for people to enjoy.

Quick Test

1. How does soil erosion affect people living downstream?

2. What methods are used to control soil erosion?

3. In what ways do forests protect soils and prevent flooding?

Answers 1. Washed out soil will cover downstream farmlands making them infertile. **2.** Erosion dams, forest planting, contour ploughing, stone stripes, fallowing, mulching. **3.** Trees intercept rainfall preventing rapid run-off.

Case-study: the Nile

Climate data

The Nile is considered by many people to be the longest river in the world (although some scientists now believe that the Amazon is longer). Its basin is located in several African countries: Burundi, Democratic Republic of Congo, Eritrea, Ethiopia, Rwanda, Uganda, Tanzania, Kenya, Sudan and Egypt. These are the countries of the Nile Basin Initiative, and they control and manage the waters of the Nile and its tributaries.

Nile basin

Key
● Location of climate stations

Cairo

Egypt

Aswan High Dam

Lake Nasser

Sudan

Blue Nile

Bahr Dar

White Nile

Ethiopia

Entebbe

500km

Temperature (°C)

Rainfall (mm)

Cairo
Lower Nile

Bahr Dar
Blue Nile

Entebbe
White Nile

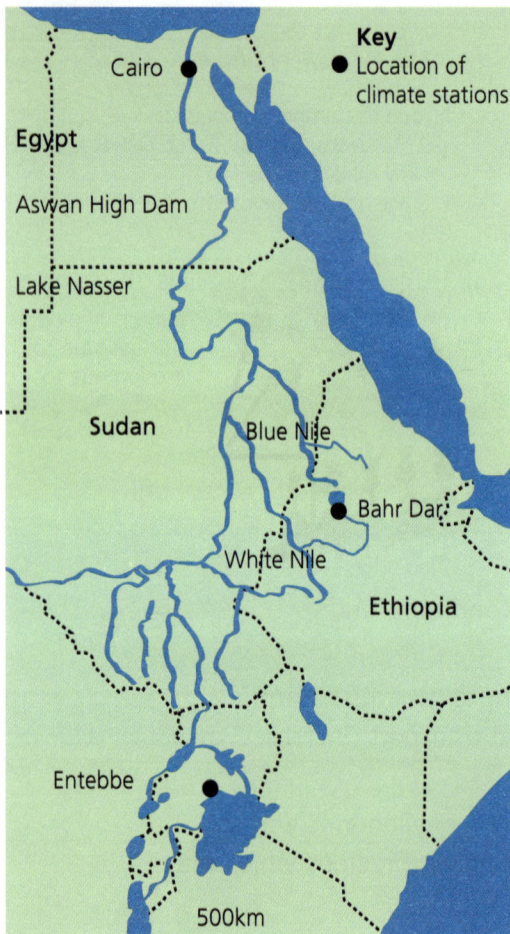

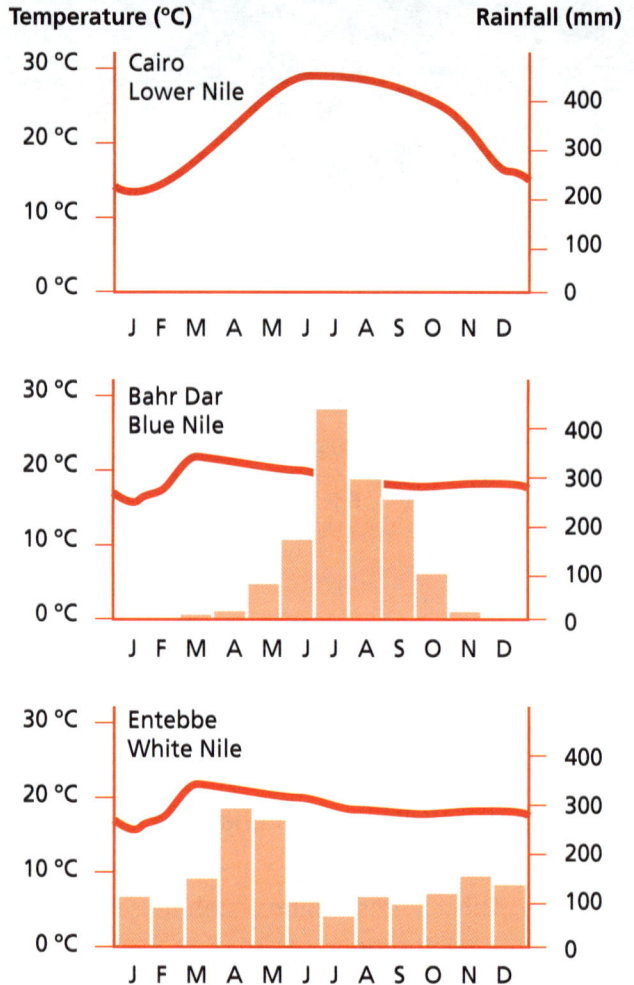

Climate Analysis

The map shows the course of the River Nile from source to mouth. The Cairo climate graph shows that Egypt has a desert climate: the rainfall is too low to support a river like the Nile. The great volume of water that passes by Cairo comes from Lake Victoria and the Ethiopian Highlands far to the south. Here, heavy seasonal rain provides the reliable water supply that once flooded the Nile Valley for several months of the year. The climate graphs for the Blue Nile at Bahr Dar and the White Nile at Entebbe show the rainfall responsible for the floods.

Landscapes along the Nile

There are many landscapes along the Nile: rainforests, savannah grasslands, mountain ranges in Ethiopia, lakes, swamps and deserts. The lower Nile is dominated by desert and the river has cut a low lying flood plain. Water is stored in the permeable rocks of the Nile basin, creating an underground water store that helps to recharge the river as it flows.

Harnessing the Nile

Egypt has a population of 82 million. This has grown from 35 million in 1970. This is rapid population growth. Most of the population depend on the Nile and most live along its banks.

Between the 1950s and 1970s the Aswan High Dam was built across the Nile for a number of reasons.

- To **control** the annual **floods** and prevent flood damage
- To provide a **reliable water supply** and avoid drought
- To store the flood water in the massive **Lake Nasser**
- To produce huge quantities of **hydroelectric power** (HEP) for industrial development and to provide energy to towns and cities along the Nile
- To create large **irrigation schemes** to help cultivate more land and feed the growing population.

Top Tip
Quote these figures in your exam answer to show population growth: Egypt CBR 22 per 1000, CMR 6 per 1000.

Farming and irrigation

The Aswan High Dam Project has improved farming. Egypt's climate gives a 12 month growing season when crops are irrigated. Three crops per year can be produced on **irrigated land**. New technology is being used to make the most of the water available. Circulating **sprayer booms** automatically water fields and modern **drip feed systems** not only supply water but also provide the correct dose of fertiliser. Ultra-modern, American-style **feed lots** rear cattle for meat and dairy products. Farming is becoming increasingly hi-tec but small scale farmers also benefit from being able to export their crops or sell them in the growing urban areas.

Problems

However, a number of problems have occurred in the area as a result of the construction of the dam:

- Previously, the Nile floods carried silt downstream and this helped to fertilise the soil below the dam. Farmers now rely on expensive fertilisers that they have to buy.
- Fishing downstream of the dam has been ruined.
- Silting is reducing the depth of the reservoir.
- Flood waters no longer flush salt out of the Nile Delta lands, reducing the crops produced.
- People were displaced by the dam and reservoir and Ancient Egyptian sites were flooded.

Overall benefits

The Aswan High Dam Project has allowed Egypt to develop into a modern democratic state. It has allowed increased agricultural production, and cheap HEP has encouraged industrial development in the urban areas. This has provided many jobs and led to economic development. Egypt cooperates with other Nile countries in deciding how the water resources of the region are to be shared. This management of limited water resources has made Egypt a relatively stable country politically.

European environmental inequalities

The context for this topic is Europe where there are many countries, all at different levels of development. There is great variety in physical landscapes, climate and social and economic activities. The European Union (EU) and national governments produce a range of policies dealing with the environment. You will have covered case-studies in class from mainland Europe and other parts. You should concentrate on these and compare them to the general points given here.

European environmental concerns

- **Air quality** is an important issue. Clean air is a basic right, but air pollution from towns, industries and traffic has a big impact on the quality of life of many people. Poor air quality leads to medical conditions like asthma and lung disease. **Smog** causes damage to buildings and creates acid rain. Burning fossil fuels is linked to global warming and environmental change.
- **Rivers** play a key role in the lives of most Europeans. Flood risks have to be managed and pollution of water has to be controlled to protect the environment and to create sustainable water supplies.
- **Sea and coastal areas** contain important sensitive ecosystems and are a resource for many people who depend on them for a living.
- **Mountain areas** tend to be remote and relatively undeveloped. They are coming under pressure, however, particularly from leisure and recreation activities such as skiing and mountaineering.

Environmental issues

Environmental factor	Issues involved
Population densities affect the quality of the environment.	High population densities create overcrowding problems and affect water and air quality. Large numbers of visitors have a negative effect on environmentally sensitive areas like mountains and coastal resorts.
Transport development	Transport developments allow access to remote and unspoiled areas. This has effects on conservation. Rivers are main transport routes as well as important ecosystems. This can lead to pollution and conflict.
Physical and climatic environments are under pressure.	Climate and land use change affects the natural environment. Sustainable development is required to protect the interests of nature and to ensure employment and leisure opportunities in the future.
Economic activity must be sustainable.	Industry, farming, tourism and settlement create pressure on land and water resources. The long term costs and benefits need to be planned into developments.
Living standards	Inequalities in living standards are being reduced by the EU policies. Development and increased consumption put pressure on the natural environment.
Environmental protection	Governments have responsibilities to ensure that they control use of the environment in such a way that they cooperate with other nations in maintaining environmental quality.

Environmental case-studies

Differences in environmental quality

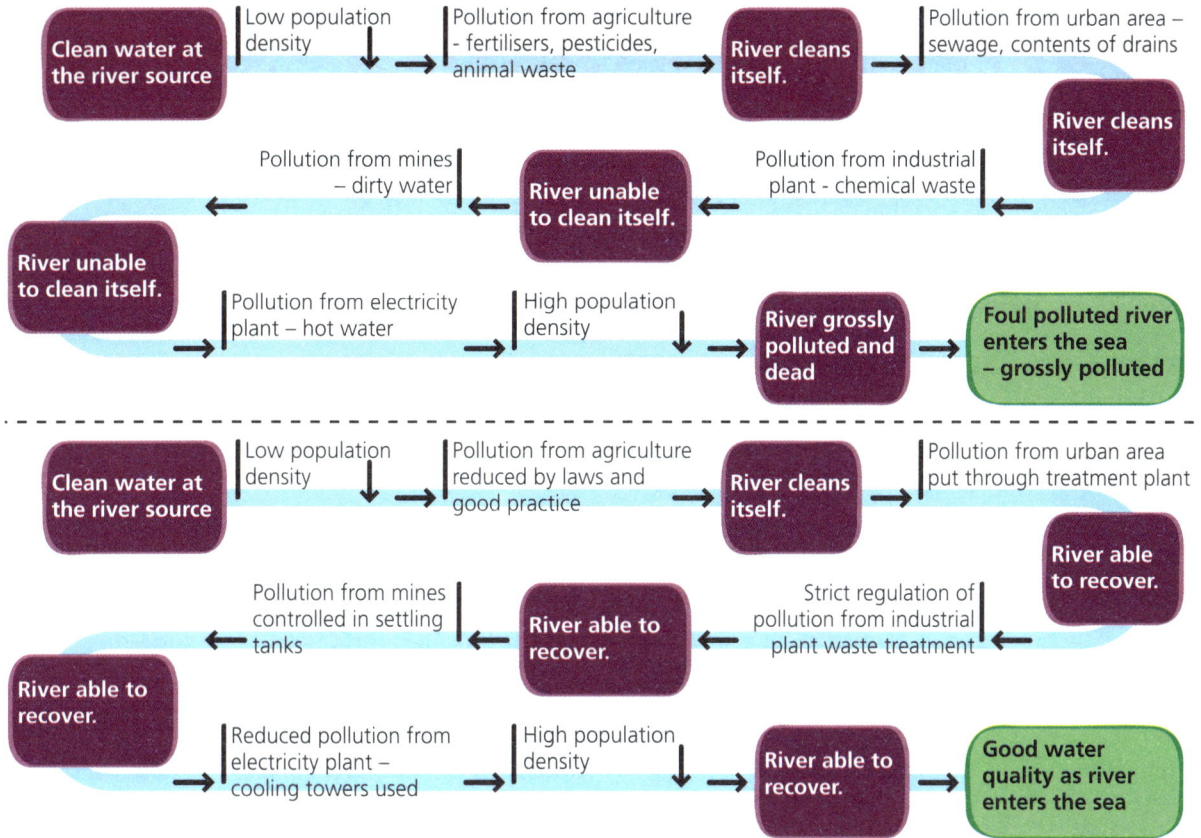

Clean water at the river source →	Low population density ↓ →
Pollution from agriculture - fertilisers, pesticides, animal waste →	**River cleans itself.** →
Pollution from urban area – sewage, contents of drains ↓	

River cleans itself. ←

Pollution from industrial plant - chemical waste ←

River unable to clean itself. ← Pollution from mines – dirty water ←

River unable to clean itself.

Pollution from electricity plant – hot water → High population density ↓ → **River grossly polluted and dead** → **Foul polluted river enters the sea – grossly polluted**

- -

Clean water at the river source → Low population density ↓ → Pollution from agriculture reduced by laws and good practice → **River cleans itself.** → Pollution from urban area put through treatment plant ↓

River able to recover. ←

Strict regulation of pollution from industrial plant waste treatment ←

River able to recover. ← Pollution from mines controlled in settling tanks ←

River able to recover.

Reduced pollution from electricity plant – cooling towers used → High population density ↓ → **River able to recover.** → **Good water quality as river enters the sea**

- Compare two rivers; the river flow diagrams provided will help with a short hand version of some of the problems and solutions.

- Compare two coastal or sea areas; pollution issues are similar to the river ones. Think also about the effects of oil drilling, pollution from spills from ships and pollution from holiday resort developments.

- Compare two mountain areas by looking at industrial and tourist developments.

For the study areas you have worked on, follow up on local, regional, national and international (EU) policies aimed at managing, maintaining and improving environmental quality. Compare how different European countries tackle similar or common problems. Look out for conflicts and how they are resolved.

Study other environmental interactions in this book (especially their diagrams), even if you don't have to cover them for the exam.

Quick Test

1. What are the main causes of air pollution?

2. Why are rivers important ecosystems as well as important transport routes?

3. How is the environment affected by holiday resort development along any European coastal area you have studied?

Answers 1. Vehicle exhausts, burning fossil fuels in factories and power stations. **2.** They provide wildlife habitats. **3.** Holiday resorts can create sewage and pollution while building them may destroy wildlife habitats such as wetlands and dunes.

Analysing past paper questions

European Environmental Inequalities

One way to predict the sort of questions that might be in the exam paper is to analyse past papers and look at the types of questions that crop up and the topics they typically cover. This can be done for any section of the paper but it is attempted here for European environmental inequalities to demonstrate how you might go about analysing sections of the paper.

Method for analysing topic cover

- Take the most recent past papers available and identify one question, e.g. Q5 European Regional Inequalities 2006, 2007, 2008. (For the analysis of the 2006 paper, please visit www.leckieandleckie.co.uk.)
- Read through Q5 on each paper, noting common themes.
- Create a grid to record question content and topics.
- Summarise common themes in the questions.

2007 paper Q5 european environmental inequalities

Question	Topic	Answer summary
a) (i) Describe the pattern of sulphur dioxide emissions shown on the reference map. (4 marks)	Pollution of air, uses map of Europe showing pollution by SO2 by country **Link to Q5(a) 2006**	Sulphur dioxide pollution is concentrated in • highly industrialised areas like NW Europe, e.g. industrial core areas of Germany, Belgium and the Netherlands • large cities producing vehicle emissions • power stations which use coal, oil and gas to generate electricity to supply the urban and industrial areas • old industrial areas of eastern Europe, which still have poorly performing, polluting industry
(ii) Explain the pattern described in terms of population density, transport links, living standards and industrial activity. (4 marks)	Causes of SO_2 emissions	Specific cause of pollution by SO_2 • use of fossil fuels, power generation, motor transport • industrial emissions from chemical works and factories • increased use of cars as people get richer • higher demand for electricity in wealthy developed countries of western Europe • large concentrations of population, e.g. the Randstadt, or the Paris-London-Berlin triangle
(b) (i) For any river you have studied describe the strategies used to maintain or improve water quality. (4 marks)	River pollution – describing methods to improve the environment. **Link to Q5(c)(i) 2006**	Measures involved might include • laws to prevent dumping polluted waste water • sewage treatment enforcement • controls on dumping effluent and hot water from power stations in rivers, e.g. cooling towers and settling ponds • advice to farmers to control fertiliser and pesticide use • development of environmentally protected areas such as wetlands
(ii) Comment on how effective these measures have been. (3 marks)	Summary of the effectiveness of measures put in place **Link to Q5(c)(ii) 2006**	Effectiveness of measures varies, e.g. • european governments have worked together to improve river quality, e.g. along the Rhine and Danube • many rivers are less polluted today than in the past, e.g. the Thames • polluter pays philosophy has reduced industrial pollution Europe wide

2008 Paper Q5 European Environmental Inequalities

Question	Topic	Answer summary
a) (i) Describe the variations in levels of acid rain throughout Europe (shown on the reference map). (3 marks)	Pollution of air, uses map of European countries showing levels of acid rain **Link to Q5(a) 2006, 5(a)(i) 2007**	Acid rain is more concentrated in • Highly industrialised areas like NW Europe, e.g. industrial core areas of Germany, Belgium and the Netherlands. Large cities are found here producing vehicle emissions. • Power stations use coal, oil and gas to generate electricity to supply the urban and industrial areas. • Old industrial areas of eastern Europe still have poorly performing polluting industry. • Prevailing winds appear to move the acid rain pollution eastwards across Europe.
(ii) Explain how economic activity and climate affect levels of acid rain throughout Europe (4 marks)	Causes of acid rain related to human activity and to weather features **Link to Q5(a)(ii) 2007**	Specific cause of acid rain pollution See • Use of fossil fuels-power generation, motor transport • Industrial emissions from chemical works and factories • Increased use of cars as people get richer • Higher demand for electricity in wealthy developed countries of western Europe
(b) For either two sea/coastal areas or two mountain areas in Europe you have studied explain the differences in environmental quality. (4 marks)	Contrasting environmental quality **Link to Q5(c)(i) 2006**	Differences in environmental quality will depend on • Laws to protect the environment such as giving National Park or nature reserve status • Pressure of population or tourist numbers on the chosen environmental areas • Controls on waste related to tourist and economic activity • Dominant land uses in the areas • Nearness to large population centres and ease of access
(c) Giving examples, describe ways in which countries and people have cooperated to improve the quality of European rivers (4 marks)	International and national measures to control river water quality in Europe **Link Q5(b)(i) 2007**	Example might include • European governments have worked together to improve river quality along the Rhine and Danube, e.g. the International Commission for the Protection of the Rhine (ICPR). • Many rivers are less polluted today than in the past, e.g. the Thames, laws have been passed to prevent pollution but opinions have been changed by green politics.

Conclusions

The analysis of questions is useful because it reveals a number of important things about the examination paper.

• Questions often repeat themselves over a number of years so you can prepare for them specifically.
• You need to learn specific case-studies to support your answer.
• Sometimes you will be able to write well about the example provided in the paper.
• There are general factors such as the causes of pollution that are a common thread through all questions.
• You need to be able to interpret maps of Europe relating to pollution issues.

Development and health

Social and economic health indicators

There are differences in the levels of development and health of people. These are measurable using a number of **social and economic indicators** that show contrasts between EMDCs and ELDCs. Differences within countries also exist. For example, developed areas have natural resources such as minerals or oil, whereas other areas show little development due to few resources. Alternatively, there may well be differences between urban and rural areas.

Social and economic indicators

Indicator	Comment
Crude birth rate, crude mortality rate and infant mortality rate **CBR, CMR and IMR**	**Social indicators** that appear high in ELDCs due to poor living conditions and poorly developed health services.
Gross national product **GNP** per capita	One of the main **economic indicators**. This measures the total value of goods and services produced by a country in a year in $US. The higher the GNP the more economically developed a country is.
Gross domestic product **GDP** per capita	Another **economic indicator**. Preferred to GNP because it does not include earnings from such things as share dealings and the insurance market which are not such a big element in ELDCs.
% adult literacy rate	A good **social indicator** as, by showing the number of adults who can read and write in a country, it shows whether or not resources are available for education.
Energy consumption per head	An **economic indicator** that reveals high - levels of energy use in richer, more industrialised countries than in poor, less well-off ELDCs.

Other social and economic figures may be used such as the number of doctors per head of population, national income per head, or percentage urban/rural population. These figures may be produced in a table or may form the basis of a distribution map like the one below. Understanding the basis of these figures will help you to identify ELDCs and EMDCs and to rank countries in terms of economic and social development.

World GNP per capita ($US)

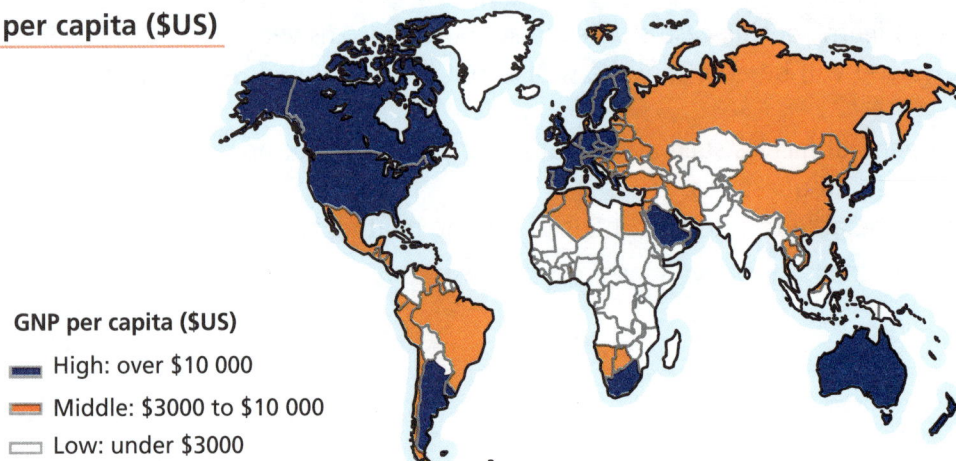

GNP per capita ($US)
- High: over $10 000
- Middle: $3000 to $10 000
- Low: under $3000

Relying on **one indicator** may prove unsatisfactory as it only looks at one factor, among many, contributing to development. For example, high GDP may be a feature of oil-producing countries like Saudi Arabia but other indicators, such as levels of literacy, may not be correspondingly high. Also, the apparent wealth might lie alongside low levels of female literacy where educational opportunities are not equal.

By using composite indicators such as PQLI (physical quality of life index) or HDI (human development index) the problems of single indicators are overcome. These measures group several indicators for each country together to form an index which makes more reliable comparisons between countries. They are less likely to be distorted by one factor such as high oil income.

Explaining differences in social and economic development

Physical factors

Climate affects development. For example, dry areas such as deserts or dry grasslands make farming difficult and discourage settlement. **Steep relief** discourages settlement, farming or communications but flatter areas do much better. **Resources** such as minerals or energy sources, e.g. oil or coal, attract settlement and provide money for the economy. Some environments are particularly challenging such as rainforests, mountain ranges or cold tundras. **Natural disasters** such as floods, earthquakes, hurricanes and volcanic eruptions can affect development.

Human factors

Demographic (population) change can affect development. For example, a **high birth rate** puts pressure on the limited economic resources needed to provide schools and health care. **Urbanisation** may be a sign of economic development tied to industrial growth, but it may also be associated with the extreme poverty of slums and shantytowns. **Industrialisation** provides jobs and encourages social and economic development. With greater industrial development comes trade and this provides cash for the economy, but sometimes countries produce goods whose prices are volatile on the world markets. **Trade** relies on the development of roads, railways and ports. The level of **technology** a country has is important in an increasingly hi-tec world.

Quick Test

1. Why are indicators such as GDP not always reliable in showing the level of development of a country?
2. Name three social indicators and three economic indicators?
3. How can natural disasters affect a county's level of development?

Answers 1. They are averages for whole countries, and there might be large gaps between rich areas and poor areas. Also, GDP doesn't show literacy or IMR, for example. **2.** Social: IMR, CBR, CMR. Economic: energy consumption per head, GDP, national income per head. **3.** Natural disasters such as earthquakes and hurricanes do huge amounts of damage to the economy by destroying buildings, roads and homes.

Disease case-study 1: heart disease

What is heart disease?

Coronary heart disease (CHD) is mostly found in EMDCs. It is caused by the arteries becoming narrowed and blocked, which reduces blood supply and oxygen to the heart. The main symptom of CHD is a condition called angina, caused by too little oxygen reaching the heart due to reduced blood flow. Heart attacks and angina are most likely to occur during or after strenuous exercise or activity.

The right side of the heart pumps blood to the lungs to be oxygenated.

The heart is mainly made of muscle.

The left side of the heart pumps blood containing nutrients and oxygen around the body.

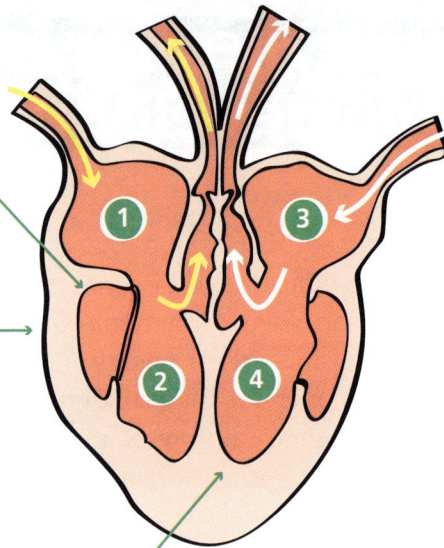

Risk factors for heart disease

The causes of heart disease are known as risk factors. Having one or more of these factors will increase the risk of a person developing heart disease.

Factors beyond normal control

Age because older people are more likely to have heart disease.
Being male because more men develop heart disease than women.
Genetic make-up because your family history of heart disease is a key risk factor.

Outside risk factors

Smoking not only constricts the body's blood vessels but also encourages the formation of blood clots that can stop blood supply to the heart. Similarly, it reduces the blood supply to the heart by damaging the lungs. Smokers also carry more carbon monoxide in their blood stream which further reduces oxygen supply.

High blood pressure causes damage to the blood vessels and heart muscle which is forced to work harder.

Top Tip
Healthy eating, drinking plenty of water and taking exercise will keep you sharp as you prepare for your exams.

High cholesterol levels in the blood lead to the build up of fatty deposits that may restrict blood flow.

Lack of physical activity limits and reduces blood supply.

Obesity and being overweight creates blood circulation problems such as fatty deposits that cause blood clots to form. It is also likely to be associated with high blood pressure and high cholesterol levels when caused by poor diet. Being overweight is also likely to result in lower levels of activity.

Other risk factors

Stress, such as stress at work or stressful situations, can promote high blood pressure or put strain on the heart.

High levels of **alcohol consumption** increase the risk of heart disease.

Top Tip
Exam stress is best avoided by thorough preparation and effective revision.

Preventing heart disease

Prevention of heart disease is best done by adopting a lifestyle that reduces the risk factors given above. Smokers are **2–3 times** more likely to die of heart disease than non-smokers. High blood pressure can be treated with modern drugs but is best prevented by healthy eating and plenty of exercise. Diet is a key element in avoiding heart disease as it affects the levels of cholesterol in the system and diets high in fat are associated with being overweight. A healthy, balanced diet containing the recommended levels of nutrients such as protein, carbohydrates, fats and vitamins will do a lot to reduce the risk factors. This is especially true if it is associated with regular exercise.

Treating heart disease

Heart disease can be treated and managed very effectively. Education is used to raise awareness of the risk factors and to encourage people to have regular check-ups relating to such things as blood pressure and cholesterol. Anti-coagulant drugs may be used to improve blood flow as might by-pass surgery. Damaged blood vessels may be replaced or blocked sections enlarged. Heart transplant surgery may be used.

Follow up activity

Check your own risk factors online.

Quick Test

1. List **four** risk factors for heart disease.
2. Why are smoking cigarettes and heart disease linked?
3. Give **two** ways to avoid heart disease.

Answers 1. Poor diet, smoking, lack of exercise, genetic factors. **2.** Smoking reduces oxygen supply to the heart. **3.** Avoid the avoidable risk factors, e.g. eat a good diet, reduce alcohol consumption.

Disease case-study 2: malaria

What is malaria?

Malaria is a widespread disease found mainly in the equatorial and tropical regions. The map below shows the distribution of malaria. It is found in large parts of Africa south of the Sahara Desert. It is also widespread in parts of south and south-east Asia as well as in Central America and the Amazon region of Brazil.

Distribution of malaria, 2007

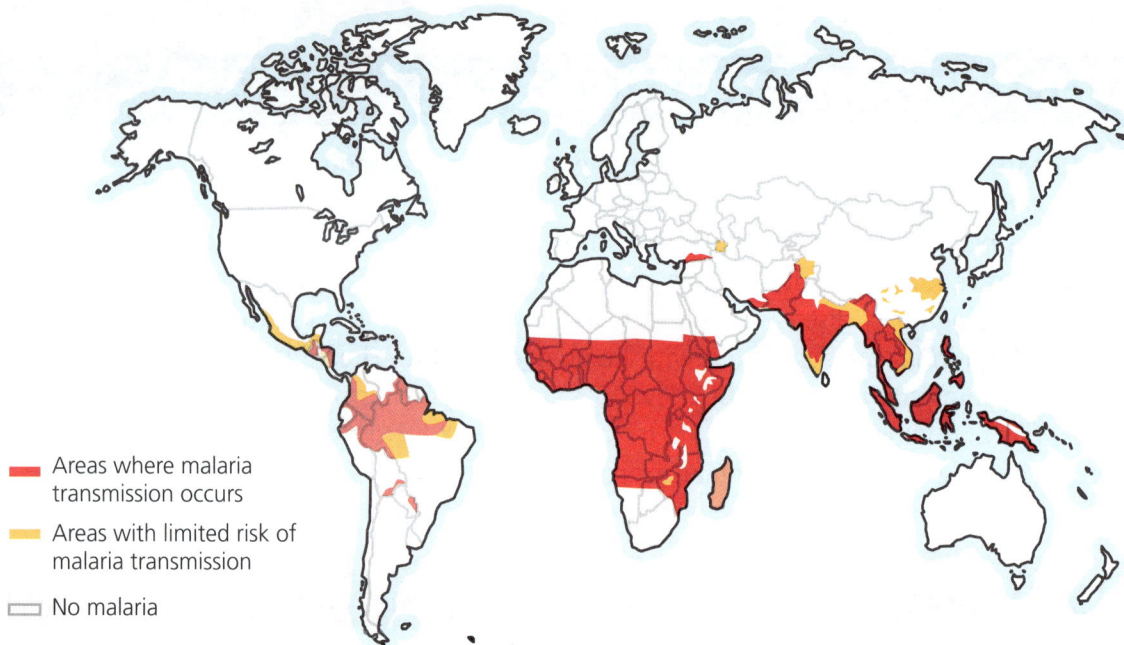

Areas where malaria transmission occurs

Areas with limited risk of malaria transmission

No malaria

The causes and effects of malaria

Malaria is caused by species of the parasite *plasmodium* and is passed from person to person by the bite of infected mosquitoes. Malaria kills over 1 million people every year, mostly young people, infants and pregnant women, and most of them in Africa and south-east Asia. The symptoms of the disease appear 10 to 15 days after the victim has been bitten by a *plasmodium*-infected mosquito. It brings on headache, fever, chills and vomiting, and if not treated early is likely to lead to death. Malaria not only makes people sick but also reduces their ability to work and so has a serious effect on the level of development in many ELDCs.

Please visit www.leckieandleckie.co.uk for a diagram showing the cycle of infection for malaria.

Environmental factors favouring mosquitoes and malaria transmission

- Temperatures in the range 21 to 27 degrees Celsius
- Relatively high rainfall totals found in tropical areas which creates stagnant water – ideal breeding grounds for mosquitoes
- People living within 3 kilometres of mosquito breeding grounds
- Disrupted landscapes with water filled pot holes and depressions such as bomb craters where pools form to provide habitat for mosquito eggs to hatch
- Untidy urban areas where any abandoned container or an old tyre, for example, could offer conditions for mosquito breeding.

Preventing malaria

Preventing malaria transmission involves a number of measures which can be used alongside malaria treatment to reduce the number of infected people in an area. Prevention mostly involves avoiding mosquito bites, controlling mosquito numbers and removing mosquito breeding grounds.

Preventative methods

Preventative method	Effectiveness
Providing bed nets	Mosquitoes are most active in the evening; sleeping under a net will stop people, especially young children, being bitten. Clothing that covers exposed skin works in a similar way as an effective barrier – relatively cheap
Window and door screens	Keeps mosquitoes out of houses and reduces exposure to the parasite
Insecticides	Sprays and mosquito coils reduce the likelihood of being bitten but are expensive. Spraying breeding grounds and shady areas where mosquitoes lie up is effective but is expensive and has to be done regularly or mosquitoes return.
Draining marshes and swamps	Reduces mosquito numbers – especially effective if done within 3 km of human settlement
Removing craters, ruts and tidying up urban breeding pools	Very effective in controlling the disease at relatively little cost
Attacking mosquito larvae by covering standing water with egg white or oil film	Prevents larvae emerging from the water as mosquitoes and effectively drowns them – high cost
Introducing mosquito larvae eating fish to water bodies	Controls mosquito numbers and provide a sound ecological solution. Also provides nutritious food to poor communities.

Treating malaria

Malaria has been eradicated from many parts of the world by preventative methods but treating malaria has proved difficult. In the last century anti-malarial drugs, such as chloroquine, were developed to treat malaria but the parasite became resistant to these drugs because their use was too widespread and not properly controlled. In the last ten years new drugs based on artemisinin are now an effective treatment and disease resistance is not a problem with this treatment.

Top Tip

Look up the World Health Organisation on the Internet and get the most up-to-date information about malaria

Follow up activity

What is the **Roll Back Malaria Campaign**?

Disease case-study 3: Acquired Immune Deficiency Syndrome (AIDS)

What is AIDS?

AIDS is an incurable condition caused by the Human Immunodeficiency Virus (HIV). This virus is in the main a sexually transmitted virus. It is passed from one person to another by the exchange of bodily fluids such as blood, semen and vaginal fluid. The virus attacks the human immune system which provides the body's natural defence against infection.

The virus is a special type of virus called a retrovirus which uses our own cells to make copies of itself. These viruses are particularly difficult to treat as they constantly mutate, that is, create different variants of themselves.

Spreading the disease

The map below shows that HIV infection is widespread across the world, particularly in the African countries that lie south of the Sahara desert, such as South Africa, Zimbabwe and Mozambique. Of the EMDCs, Russia and eastern Europe have the highest rates of infection. The World Health Organisation estimates that 33 million people worldwide are infected with HIV and that so far 25 million people have died as a result of it. In the UK it is estimated that there are 73 000 people living with HIV. The numbers of people infected by the virus continue to rise year by year.

The main way to contract the virus is through sexual intercourse, including oral and anal sex. The virus is also spread by sharing needles, blood transfusions and from pregnant women to their unborn babies. It is now possible to prevent the transmission of the virus from mother to child during pregnancy.

Distribution of HIV infection, 2008

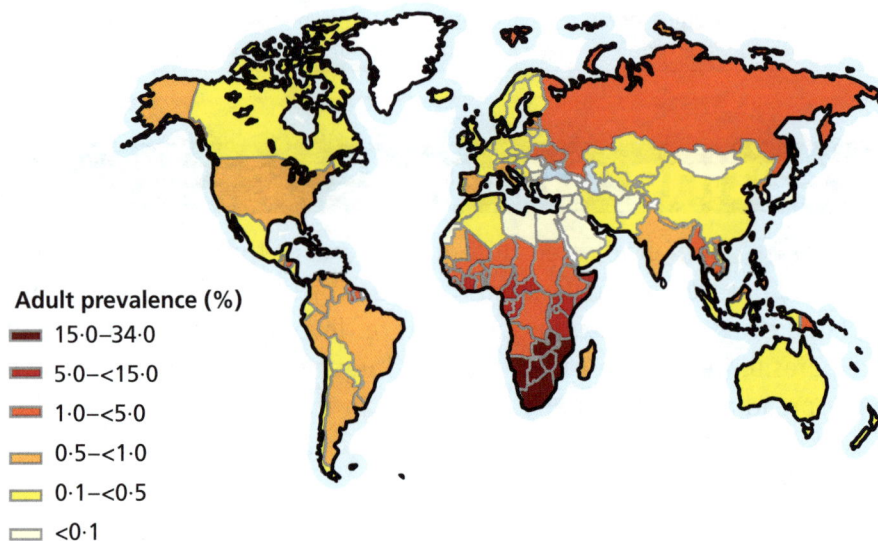

Adult prevalence (%)

- 15·0–34·0
- 5·0–<15·0
- 1·0–<5·0
- 0·5–<1·0
- 0·1–<0·5
- <0·1

You can see the statistics for 2005 at www.leckieandleckie.co.uk.

Preventing the disease

The disease is prevented by being aware of the risks it poses and avoiding the interchange of bodily fluids between people. Guidelines suggest ways to avoid contracting HIV.

- Safe sex involves using a condom and is the best way to avoid getting sexually transmitted infections (STIs) including HIV.
- Avoid having unprotected sex with multiple partners.
- Intravenous drug users should not share needles.
- Be aware that although blood transfusions in the UK are screened for HIV, this is not necessarily true in other parts of the world and they may carry a risk of infection.

Treating the disease

HIV/AIDS is incurable but the progress of the virus can be slowed by special medicines that are used in what is known as **highly active antiretroviral therapy (HAART)**. This has proved remarkably successful in slowing the progression of the condition, and prolonging life. (Source NHS Direct.)

AIDS in ELDCs: case-study Africa

The United Nations (UN) estimates that AIDS is the biggest threat to social and economic development in Africa. This is because of the large numbers of people in key roles who are dying of the disease: teachers, farmers, health workers, civil servants and young professional workers.

In ELDCs, antiretroviral therapy (HAART) is not available to the majority of people as they are too poor to be able to afford expensive drug treatment. HIV infection puts enormous strain on limited health resources. Mortality rates that have fallen for decades since the 1960s are now increasing in Sub-Saharan Africa.

Public education is seen as the most effective way of reducing the spread of HIV as experience in the EMDCs has shown. But the large numbers of deaths among education and health workers has caused obvious concern. Similarly, in countries where few children attend school and low levels of adult literacy are common, it is difficult to get the important public education messages across. Cultural practices in relation to sexual behaviour may work against the message of safe sex.

Quick Test

1. Why is HIV infection considered to be such a serious global problem?
2. What are the main ways by which HIV is transmitted from person to person?
3. How can HIV infection be avoided?
4. Why is treatment for HIV unlikely to be applied in many African states?

Answers 1. It is incurable and treatment is expensive and unavailable to most people in developing countries. **2.** Sexual contact transmission, transmission through infected blood and sharing infected needles. **3.** Safe sex, good health practice. **4.** It is too expensive for poor people.

Environmental hazards

Earthquakes and volcanoes

The map below shows the distribution of earthquakes and volcanoes. They occur along the plate boundaries where great fractures split the earth's crust into great slabs of crust called plates.

Plate boundaries, volcano and earthquake zones

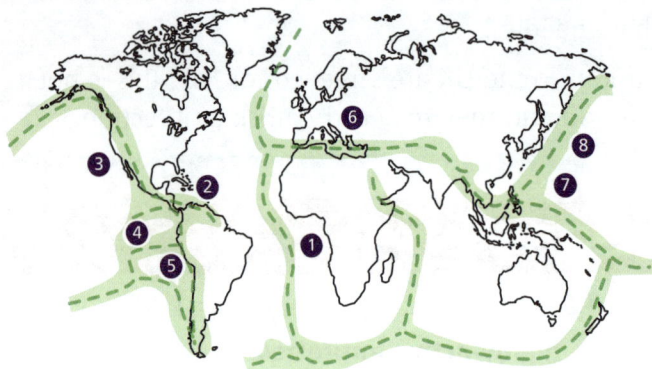

Plate and plate boundary	Volcanic or earthquake activity
1 Mid Atlantic Ridge	Atlantic volcanoes like those on Iceland, Heimaey, Surtsey
2 Caribbean Plate	Montserrat's volcano
3 Pacific coast USA	Mount St Helens, Alaskan volcanoes, San Andreas Fault California
4 Central America	Mexico City earthquakes, Nevada del Ruiz volcano disaster
5 Pacific Coast South America	Active volcanoes in the Andes mountain chain
6 Mediterranean Afro-European Plate Boundary	Vesuvius and Etna, Italian, Greek and Turkish earthquakes
7 South East Asian Plates	Mount Pinatubo massive eruption, Krakatoa, the Boxing Day Tsunami
8 South-west China	Sichuan Province earthquake 2008

Please visit www.leckieandleckie.co.uk for block diagrams showing crustal plate movements.

Top Tip

Create your own table to summarise case-studies you have used to study volcanic and earthquake activity along the plate boundaries.

Hurricanes

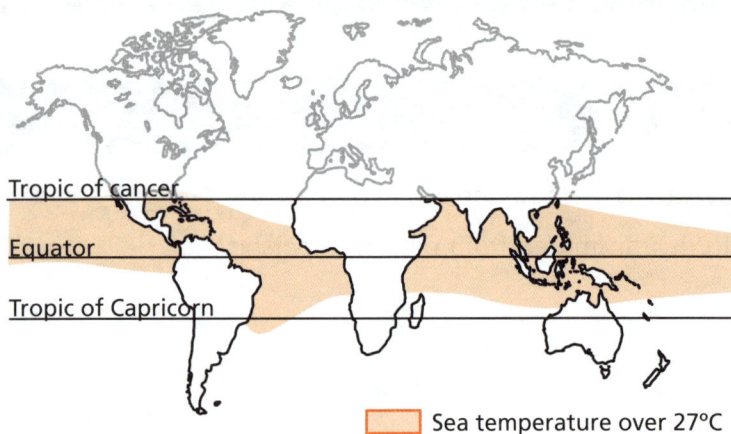

Sea temperature over 27°C

The terms hurricane and typhoon are names for a strong tropical cyclone. Tropical cyclones are deep, low-pressure systems that develop over warm tropical or sub-tropical oceans (average temperature 27 degrees Celsius). They are massive rotating storms that are high in thunderstorm activity, as convectional uplift over the warm ocean surface lifts air and the moisture it carries high into the atmosphere. When tropical cyclones hit land they bring with them high winds and heavy rainfall. They also are associated with storm surges which drive sea water inland and can have devastating consequences on low lying coastal areas such as deltas.

You should have case-study detail relating to one tropical cyclone or hurricane. You need to know the origin of the storm, where it hit and its effect on people and property. You also need to know what aid was available to help the victims of the storm and to repair the damage done.

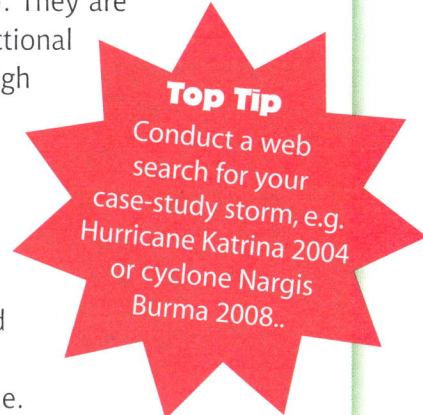

Top Tip
Conduct a web search for your case-study storm, e.g. Hurricane Katrina 2004 or cyclone Nargis Burma 2008..

Quick Test

1. Where did the storm come from?
2. What were the main weather effects associated with the storm?
3. How were people affected by the storm?

Answers 1. From the nearby ocean. **2.** High winds and heavy rain with a tidal/ocean surface storm surge. **3.** Damage to houses and property, loss of life and injuries, forced evacuation, flooding.

Disaster relief

After a major natural disaster, relief efforts kick in organised by national governments using civil defence teams or the armed forces. In addition, international aid is organised by other governments or by aid agencies such as the United Nations Disaster Relief Organisation (UNDRO) or charities such as Save the Children, OXFAM and Médecins Sans Frontières. Specialist teams may be involved using dogs or heat seeking technology to find those trapped in the debris,

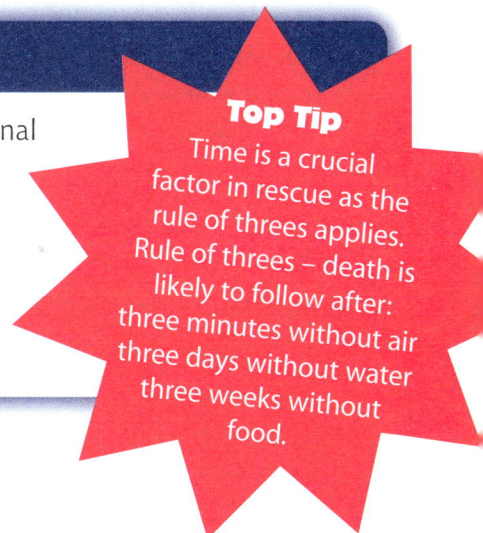

Top Tip
Time is a crucial factor in rescue as the rule of threes applies. Rule of threes – death is likely to follow after: three minutes without air three days without water three weeks without food.

Quick Test

1. Explain the distribution of earthquakes and volcanoes around the world.
2. Name some of the organisations involved in disaster relief and suggest the sort of help they might provide to an area hit by a natural disaster.
3. What is the rule of threes?

Answers 1. They are mostly on or next to plate boundaries. Name the specific plates for detail in your answer. **2.** Examples might be: Save the Children, Oxfam, UNDRO (the UN Disaster Relief Organisation). They provide emergency shelters, medical aid and food aid. **3.** It says how long you can survive without air (3 mins), water (3 days) and food (3 weeks).

Environmental hazards case-studies

Developing answer plans

Short answer plans can be used to help you revise. In the exam, answer plans can be jotted down on the paper to help you collect your thoughts before attempting your answer. This section provides examples of answer plans relating to typical hazards case-studies.

1. Asian Tsunami, Boxing Day, 2004
   - Colliding plates, subduction, earthquake, seabed moved, tsunami

2. Hurricane Katrina, 2005
   - Satellite tracking/photographs, roads crowded, poor no place to go, property worries, Mississippi/Lake Pontchartrain flood, levees broke, emergency services ineffective

3. Hurricane Katrina
   - Police looters, Louisiana Superdome, poor, dead, injured, national guard, relief, FEMA (Federal Emergency Management Agency)

4. Montserrat, West Indies, 1995
   - Plymouth evacuated, exclusion zone, 19 people died, pyroclastic flows, mud flows

5. Asian Tsunami
   - UNDRO, UNESCO, OXFAM, international rescue efforts, dogs, tents, food, water, medicine

Expanding the answer plan

1. **Hurricane Katrina**

    Warnings given about Hurricane Katrina were effective to a degree. Satellites were able to track the hurricane as it developed out in the Atlantic. (1) The US weather service used aircraft and buoys at sea to measure the storm's intensity. (1) Warnings were issued to evacuate low lying coasts and parts of New Orleans. (1) Poor people were unable to find alternative accommodation or transport out of the city so the evacuation was not effective. Poor river defences failed, but scientists had predicted it. Adequate flood defences were too expensive for the US government. (1)

Task

Try to expand each of the answer plans above into scoring answers.

Complete your own answer plans too.

Top Tip

If you run short of time short answer plans will score marks and are certainly better than leaving questions unanswered.

Answers to exam-style questions

Page 27

(i) Waterfalls can occur where hard rock and softer rock, in layers, are crossed by the river. The hard rock, e.g. volcanic dolerite, on top of the softer rock, e.g. limestone, resists erosion by the river. (1) The softer rock is undermined by the river using hydraulic action, attrition and corrasion to erode the rock. (1) A lip of hard rock hangs above the undermined soft layer and eventually it can no longer support itself so it collapses. (1) The debris is swirled around in the plunge pool below the waterfall which is how this feature becomes deeper. (1) (A diagram with annotations may be included.)

(ii) Meanders are caused by the turbulent flow of a river which has a side to side motion. (1) Rivers, their valleys and banks erode using hydraulic action and corrasion. (1) In a meander the outsides of the bends are eroded as they are undercut by the fast-flowing water on the outside of the bend. (1) Deposition of sediment takes place on the inside of the bend where the speed of flow is less. (1) Meanders cut into themselves and this may lead to the formation of oxbow lakes where the river breaks through the narrowing neck of the meander. (1) (An annotated diagram will make it easier to explain this feature.)

Page 37

1. There are many tourist related activities shown on the map, for example the ski area 995054 is an important part of the local economy. (1) It provides many jobs managing the slopes as well as in the shops in Aviemore 893118. (1) The National Mountaineering Training Centre 986093 and the Cairngorm corries 985026 show that mountaineering provides similar income to local people. (1) Skiing and mountaineering can have an environmental impact, for example the funicular railway and the ski tows create a visual intrusion. (1) Climbers and walkers create footpath erosion on the hillsides. (1) Visitors may be attracted to honeypots such as the Loch Morlich water sports centre 972098; this may cause overcrowding and disturbance to wildlife. (1) Visitors to the Glenmore Forest Park 9710 may cause damage to trees by lighting fires (1) or may disturb wildlife with dogs or mountain bike activities. (1)

2(a) The River Allt Creag an Leth-choin rises at 1050 metres and flows NE to Coire an Lochan. At 981030 it turns due South to a junction with a tributary at 980062. The river is in its upper course because of the steep relief. It flows through a steep sided gorge at 985067 again typical of the upper course. It has many small meanders along its course (square 9806). Having turned in a westerly direction at 985091 it enters Loch Morlich though a small delta at 970092.

(b) 964026 **U-shaped valley**
981028 **corrie and lochan**
988035 **arête**
004026 **hanging valley**

(c) Corries form on cold north facing slopes in hollows where snow collected during the ice age. As it accumulated it turned to glacier ice and began to slide downhill due to gravity. The ice eroded the hollow deeper and deeper using plucking where the ice tore away the bedrock it was wrapped around as it moved and by abrasion using rock fragments like sandpaper to wear away the rock. After the ice age the deep armchair shaped hollow was left and rain water trapped in its bottom formed the lochan called a tarn.

(d) **A** Forest track
B River
C Forest edge
D Ski area
E Fiacaill a' Coire Cais

(e)(i) There are a wide range of leisure and tourist features on the map. Skiing is found at 994054, water sports at Loch Morlich 971098. The forest is used for mountain biking with a cycle track at 978080. The camping ground and youth hostel in 9709 provide accommodation.

(ii) Leisure and tourism are important to the local economy as tourists spend money in the shops and hotels in Aviemore. Visitors create employment for local people and the ski industry keeps the economy going in the winter. These jobs help to prevent out migration from this mountainous area and maintain the population of the area. Many people can get jobs in outdoor activities such as at the National Outdoor Training centre 985093. Skilled jobs are created working for bodies like the National Park Authority as a conservationist and these attract a higher rate of pay.

Index